Landscape History
Discoveries in the
North West

Sharon Varey   Graeme White

Alan Crosby   John Whithall

Mike Shadow   Stewart Ainsworth

Dan Morgan Evans   Graeme White

John Lowe

Landscape History Discoveries in the North West

Proceedings of a Conference
sponsored by English Heritage
to celebrate the 25th Anniversary of the
Chester Society for Landscape History,
September 2011

Edited by **Sharon M. Varey** and **Graeme J. White**

With an Introduction by **Dai Morgan Evans**

University of Chester Press

First published 2012
by University of Chester Press
Parkgate Road
Chester CH1 4BJ

Printed and bound in the UK by the
LIS Print Unit
University of Chester
Cover designed by the LIS Graphics Team
University of Chester

A catalogue record of this book is available
from the British Library

ISBN 978-1-908258-00-7

CONTENTS

LIST OF COLOUR PLATES

PICTURE ACKNOWLEDGEMENTS

Paper 1: Ainsworth, Stanlow Abbey
Figure 1: English Heritage © Crown Copyright and database right 2009. All rights reserved. Ordnance Survey Licence 100019088.
Figures 5–9: English Heritage © and database right Crown Copyright and Landmark Information Group Ltd (All rights reserved) Licence numbers 000394 and TP0024.
Figure 10: Crown Copyright. All rights reserved. Ordnance Survey licence number 100019088. Reproduced with the permission of Cheshire Archives and Local Studies.
Plate 1: English Heritage © Crown Copyright and database right 2009. All rights reserved. Ordnance Survey Licence 100019088.
Plate 3: Based on lidar © Environment Agency.

Paper 2: Annakin, Curvilinear Enclosures
Figure 3: Used with kind permission of Rob Philpott. © Merseyside Museums.
Plate 4: 1983–85 Aerial Survey of North and East Cheshire. Copyright Cheshire West & Chester Council and Cheshire East Council © All rights reserved.

Paper 3: Headon, Settlements and their Shapes
Figures 3–4 and 6–7: Detail reproduced from the Digital Archives Association DVD Ordnance Survey 6-inch First Edition Maps of Flintshire and Denbighshire 1869–75, with their permission.
Figure 5: By permission of Llyfrgell Genedlaethol Cymru/The National Library of Wales: John Thomas Photographic Collection, JTH00502.

Picture Acknowledgements

Plate 5: Image reproduced by permission of Clwyd-Powys Archaeological Trust (CPAT image 1766-370).

Paper 4: White, The Enclosure of West Cheshire
Figure 1: CALS: DDX 27/2, reproduced by permission of Cheshire Archives and Local Studies and the owner/depositor to whom copyright is reserved.
Figure 2: Copyright 2006 Cheshire West & Chester Council and Cheshire East Council ©. All rights reserved. Flown and captured by Hunting Surveys Ltd, 8 July 1971.
Figure 3: English Heritage. NMR RAF Photography as supplied by Cheshire West & Chester Council, image captured 17 January 1947.
Figure 5: CALS: QDE 2/1, reproduced by permission of Cheshire Archives and Local Studies and the owner/depositor to whom copyright is reserved.
Plate 6: Enclosure map: Baker-Wilbraham family deeds, CALS: DBW M/M/E no. 3, reproduced by permission of Cheshire Archives and Local Studies and the owner/depositor to whom copyright is reserved. Aerial photograph reproduced by permission of Cheshire West & Chester Council and Cheshire East Council © 2009; flown and captured by National Remote Sensing Centre Ltd, 1992–93; digitally converted by Bluesky International Ltd., 2009.
Plate 7: Image supplied by Bluesky © GeoPerspectives.

Paper 5: Whittle, A Description and History of Walk Mill
Figure 2: Reproduced by permission of National Museums, Liverpool.
Figure 4: Reproduced by permission of Dr A.J.P. Campbell.
Figure 6: Reproduced by permission of Cheshire Archives and Local Studies and the owner/depositor to whom copyright is reserved.

Figure 7: English Heritage. NMR RAF Photography as supplied by Cheshire West & Chester Council, image captured 17 January 1947.
Figure 9: Reproduced by permission of Mr Ben Jones, owner of Walk Mill.

Paper 8: Swailes, An East Cheshire Township in Transition
Figures 1, 5, 7–8 and 10: Reproduced with permission from Bollington Civic Society archive.
Figures 2 and 9: Reproduced by permission of Cheshire Archives and Local Studies and the owner/depositor to whom copyright is reserved.

In Brief: Cox, The Rise and Fall of Llanbedr Hall
Figure 2: Reproduced by permission of Denbighshire Record Office.

In Brief: Lowe, Dawpool Hall Estate, Thurstaston, Wirral
Figure 1: Reproduced by permission of Ian and Marilyn Boumphrey.

ABBREVIATIONS

Bryant, *Map* (1831): A. Bryant, *Map of the County Palatine of Chester from an actual survey in the years 1829, 1830 and 1831* (1831)

CALS: Cheshire Archives and Local Studies

CBA: Council for British Archaeology

Ches.Hist.: *Cheshire History*

CRO: Cheshire Record Office

CSLH: Chester Society for Landscape History

HER: Historic Environment Record [that for Cheshire is now hosted by Cheshire West and Chester Council]

HMSO: Her Majesty's Stationery Office

JCAS: *Journal of the Chester Archaeological Society*

JMAS: *Journal of the Merseyside Archaeological Society*

ME: Middle English

nd: not dated

OE: Old English

ON: Old Norse

OS: Ordnance Survey

RCHM: Royal Commission on Historical Monuments

RSLC: Record Society of Lancashire and Cheshire

SA: Shropshire Archives

ser.: series

TLCAS: *Transactions of the Lancashire and Cheshire Antiquarian Society*

THSLC: *Transactions of the Historic Society of Lancashire and Cheshire*

TNA: The National Archives

VCH Ches: *Victoria History of the County of Chester*, ed. B.E. Harris, C.P. Lewis and A.T. Thacker (Oxford and Woodbridge, 1979–2005)

VCH Lancs: *Victoria History of the County of Lancaster*, ed. W. Farrer and J. Brownbill (London, 1906–14)

VCH Shrops: *Victoria History of Shropshire*, ed. W. Page, A.T. Gaydon, G.C. Baugh and C.R.J. Currie (London and Oxford, 1908–98)

NOTES ON CONTRIBUTORS

Stewart Ainsworth is a senior archaeological investigator with the English Heritage Research Department. A long-time Chester resident, he is well-known as Channel 4's 'Time Team' landscape archaeologist and map specialist. He is co-author of *Chester Amphitheatre: From Gladiators to Gardens* (2005).

Anthony Annakin-Smith is a graduate of the MA in Landscape, Heritage and Society and an active member of the Chester Society for Landscape History. He is a lecturer and writer who became interested in the subject to try to satisfy his curiosity during country walks and has used some of his knowledge to write the popular book *Wirral Walks.*

Alan Crosby is one of Britain's most prominent local historians: editor of *The Local Historian* and a main contributor to the BBC *Who Do You Think You Are?* magazine. He is an honorary research fellow at the Universities of Lancaster and Liverpool, and was co-author of the English Heritage volume on *England's Landscape: the North West* (2006). Among his other books are *A History of Cheshire* (1996) and *A History of Warrington* (2002).

Mike Headon is a retired higher education lecturer. He is a graduate of the MA in Landscape, Heritage and Society. He is particularly interested in place-names and the landscape history of Wales. Mike is Secretary to the Chester Society for Landscape History and a key member of its Planning Team.

Dai Morgan Evans worked for the Inspectorate of Ancient Monuments and Historic Buildings and then English Heritage before becoming General Secretary of the Society of Antiquaries of London. He is Visiting Professor in Archaeology at the University of Chester and makes frequent television appearances in archaeology programmes.

Tom Swailes is a part-time university lecturer and has published work on several aspects of civil engineering history. He is a Kerridge Ridge and Ingersley Vale volunteer carrying out historic landscape conservation and management work, as well as being a member of the Chester Society for Landscape History.

Sharon Varey is a researcher and tutor. Having gained an MA in Landscape, Heritage and Society, she went on to complete a PhD on the changing landscape of Baschurch, a parish in northwest Shropshire. Sharon is currently Publications Editor and Chair of the Chester Society for Landscape History.

Graeme White is Emeritus Professor of Local History at the University of Chester and President of the Chester Society for Landscape History, having launched the Diploma in Landscape History (later to become the MA in Landscape, Heritage and Society) at what was then Chester College in 1978. Among his publications is *The Medieval English Landscape, 1000–1540* (2012).

John Whittle is a retired research scientist. An active local historian and member of the Chester Society for Landscape History, John has written a number of articles for *Cheshire History* and edited several books on his local area. He is a graduate of the MA in Landscape, Heritage and Society.

Vanessa Greatorex, Julie Smalley and John Lowe are also graduates of the MA in Landscape, Heritage and Society and, like **Rod Cox**, active members of the Chester Society for Landscape History. Vanessa Greatorex facilitates the Society's Field-Names Research Group, while Julie Smalley is Lifelong Learning Co-ordinator.

EDITORS' PREFACE

This book is the outcome of a conference entitled *25 in 2011: Landscape Discoveries in the North West*, which was held to celebrate the 25th anniversary of the Chester Society for Landscape History (CSLH) on 10 September 2011. The conference was organised by a sub-committee of the Society and attracted support and sponsorship from the University of Chester and English Heritage. Held in the conference facilities at Ness Gardens, Wirral, the aim was to bring together and celebrate the work of both amateur and professional landscape historians active in the region. By common consent, the conference was a great success and thanks must be extended to the sub-committee for the hours they put into organising the event and to the numerous members of the Society who helped out on the day.

CSLH was set up in 1986 as a direct result of the Landscape History courses – first a Diploma then a Masters – run by Chester College, which later became the University of Chester, and it is fitting that this institution has published a volume to which a number of its former students have contributed. The Society's logo, which can be seen on the cover of this publication, attracts comment for the curious reversed letter 'S' which reflects the sinuous curve of medieval open-field strips. The name signifies a landscape history society based in Chester but interested in landscape development in its broadest context. Activities have grown as the membership has increased and currently consists of lectures, field visits, study breaks, 'Discovery Days' to enhance skills, and involvement in research projects. The Field-Names Research Group is one such project featured within this publication and individual mention must be given to those members who contributed to the paper: Vanessa Greatorex, Ann Daley, Mike Headon, David Kennils,

Breta Lloyd, Tom Swailes, Mike Taylor and John Whittle. In recent years the Society has endeavoured to publish the results of members' research and alongside several booklets produces a substantial bi-annual newsletter entitled *Landscape History Today: the Bulletin of CSLH.*

The research carried out by Stewart Ainsworth, upon which his paper in this publication is based, followed a CSLH visit to Stanlow Abbey in June 2010. The visit was organised by Carmen Johnson, a longstanding member of the Society who invited English Heritage representatives to accompany CSLH members on the visit to the site. Sadly, Carmen died shortly after the visit; this paper is therefore a fitting memory to her endeavours to see the site properly recorded for posterity.

The nature of landscape research is such that many individuals are often involved in piecing together a picture of the past. The contributors are very grateful, therefore, to the staff at numerous record offices, landowners, custodians and others too numerous to mention individually, who have facilitated their research. The help and support of the University of Chester Press, especially Sarah Griffiths, in seeing the volume through to publication, is also much appreciated. Last, but by no means least, the contributors would particularly like to thank friends and family members whose help and support has been greatly valued during the months of research, writing and editing of this collection.

Sharon M. Varey and Graeme J. White (April 2012)

INTRODUCTION

Dai Morgan Evans

Landscape History?

If you are reading this Introduction, wondering what this volume is all about, you might be questioning what on earth is meant by 'landscape history'? Later in this Introduction I will briefly consider where I believe we can find the origin of the concept of 'landscape history' but in the meantime what does it mean today? Is it the same as 'landscape archaeology', how does it relate to 'local history' and even what about 'landscape gardening'? Well, like all useful concepts this one is a bit amorphous, a bit fuzzy around the edges. Much can, and has been written on the concept of landscape but essentially it is a large 'artificial' artefact created, managed and changed by human beings over hundreds, if not a few thousands of years. And it has been, and vitally for us as humans, continues to be subject to change. This dynamic applies just as much in the countryside as in urban environments. So the landscape we see today is multi-period and this inevitably means that in order to study it we have to be multi-disciplinary. This can involve work on documents, sometimes in languages other than English and all too often in bad handwriting or torn, stained or incomplete records. It also – importantly – involves fieldwork, sometimes using the records of others or getting wet and muddy ourselves: after all we are studying a very real landscape. Maps are a mainstay, air-photographs can help and technologies are always advancing and becoming more accessible – as Stewart Ainsworth demonstrated in his keynote conference address showing the wonders of lidar. Of course it is very difficult for any one person to be proficient in all the disciplines and techniques that are available and needed. This is where the existence of a group of people – a Society – helps as knowledge and experience can be shared. And as for definitions? 'Landscape history' is history, archaeology, geography, economics, botany, culture, gardening and on and on. Complex? Yes, but with a will to learn and importantly a willingness to teach and share, the joy of being able to 'read' and understand a landscape, or elements within it is, as these papers show, very rewarding.

What we owe William Camden

At this conference the Chester Society for Landscape History (CSLH) was celebrating its 25th anniversary. The Society was founded in 1986. Four hundred years earlier, in 1586, a revolutionary book was published, the author William Camden (1551–1623). This was called *Britannia,* or to give it its fuller title *a Chorographical Description of the most flourishing kingdoms of England, Scotland and Ireland and the adjacent islands from the depth of antiquity.* Well not quite in that form as the text was in Latin and remained so until 1610 and its first translation into English.[1] What has this to do with a 25th anniversary conference on Wirral of a local landscape history society? Well, everything, for the impetus for research and work that was being discussed at the conference, and which appears in this publication, can be traced back to Camden's 'revolution', and is arguably part of a process which has been under way for over four hundred years. Why do I wish to emphasis Camden at the expense of W.G. Hoskins as the 'founding parent'? Well, Hoskins, while undoubtedly *one* of the greats, was also limited in his vision. He may have attached so much importance to the visual (as opposed to documentary) evidence revealed by fieldwork that he devoted two chapters of his *Local History in England* to it.[2] However, he excluded prehistoric archaeology altogether. 'This is a distinct branch of knowledge with techniques of its own that require a specialised training for their use ...', although he admitted that in some places 'one cannot separate the history from the prehistory'. And, in the preface to the first edition in 1959, he excluded the local history of Wales and London. While a Chester society might not be expected to study London it is good to see that the border is porous and that Wales is not excluded.

But what can Camden be seen to stand for? First his work was history, based not primarily on *chron*ology but on *chor*ology. This is essentially a geographical concept involving the study of phenomena in terms of spatial relationships or areas and in an holistic way – Camden also sought to be inclusive in his material – anyone for landscape archaeology? Another important aspect can be seen in the number of editions of *Britannia* following on from the small un-illustrated 1586 version and the way it physically grew in size, detail and pictures up until the Gough edition of 1789. Camden always intended his publication to be a 'work in progress' and so it was for 200 years. In making this 'work in progress' people were invited to contribute new material or revisions of that already existing. In its own way this conference publication carries on in the tradition of Camden. Lastly Camden's *Britannia* was 'political'. Camden worked and studied within a group based around Lord Burghley and was encouraged by this group to produce *Britannia* and to continue revising it. But the work had a major role in describing and defining, in unsettled and changing times, the 'new Britain' of the Elizabethan and early Stuart monarchies. In a very real sense the papers published in this volume are founded on the approaches pioneered by William Camden 400 years ago and have a continued contemporary relevance.

The Papers

This volume contains in all twelve contributions, eight major papers and four short ones based on poster presentations at the Conference. I have selected some broad themes which seem to me to emerge from all these papers. These themes are by no means exhaustive and they are set out in no particular order. The one paper which does not easily fit into any category is that by **Julie Smalley**, Lifelong Learning Co-ordinator. This activity is a vital part of the Society's activities, as I hope has already been made clear, and as such will be emphasised again in the last section of this Introduction.

Buildings and their Landscape

This emerges as one of the numerically larger themes. Perhaps this is not surprising as buildings or structures usually represent the most culturally sophisticated element in a landscape and in terms of resources the most demanding. **Stewart Ainsworth** in his study of Stanlow Abbey gave the very clear justification why further study was necessary, and this acts as a useful reminder of one of the reasons why we continue to research and revise. He says that he focused 'on providing an informed analysis of the scheduled monument to underpin future management and conservation of the site'. If we don't understand what we have of a nationally important monument, how can we make proper decisions about it, academic or practical? But there is the further point that we need to research the later histories of the site in detail if we are to have any chance of understanding the earlier. The Stanlow Abbey site must be one of the most difficult in the country to survey and Stewart's paper is a text book example of the combination of resources, especially maps and photographs, used in working out the complex history of a much exploited peninsula.

Introduction

John Whittle's work on the Foulk Stapleford Walk Mill shares some of the same problems, but on a different, smaller scale with easier access. It is good to see that even at this scale the study area is geographically and geologically located within the wider area. What is also useful here is the summary of the early (including prehistoric) activity in the area. The fact that human activity, some of it high status, has been affecting this area of the Gowy valley for such a long period, should cause us to think carefully about the sort of landscapes that later humans found themselves responding to. But this landscape stands out as an example of the ever changing nature of the resource, with in this case, a corn mill which was demolished in 1960, not having worked for some 45 years, being recently rebuilt and back in use grinding corn. Amongst the shorter contributions there were two on buildings and their landscapes. One is by **Rod Cox** on Llanbedr Hall, another by **John Lowe** on Dawpool Hall. Both show the effect of 'imported' urban wealth on rural buildings and landscapes and the significant effect that such resources have on landscapes and communities, especially when combined with autocratic power. Interestingly both papers conclude in a modern context, Lowe rejoicing in the conversion of a diverted railway line to a cycle track, Cox with a rather dark prophecy about the widening dependency of rural economies upon essentially ephemeral urban money.

Boundaries

Reconstructing boundaries can be a dangerous occupation. There is the awful example of the way that ley lines can be constructed with the use of a map, a ruler and the ability to accept large margins of error. On the other hand much can be missed if the imagination is not allowed some latitude. **Anthony Annakin-Smith** on Curvilinear Enclosures has tackled this problem in an exemplary manner, first attempting

5

to define the structures within the landscape and then to consider and interpret them in a wider context. It is one of those truisms that you only find what you are looking for. While 'economy of hypothesis' looks more to medieval origins for these features, it is worth noting that in some parts of England Romano-British influences have been considered. It needs to be remembered that even when a farmed landscape has been abandoned, later re-occupation can make extensive use of earlier features. Curvilinear structures undoubtedly exist at Willaston but this paper is admirably honest that it is, at the moment, difficult to substantiate the interpretations offered. The exciting point is that there is a pressing invitation to do more work on this potential type of feature and that this can be very much considered as 'work in progress'.

Graeme White on Enclosures in West Cheshire bravely tackles what the *Atlas of Rural Settlement* calls 'a challenging sub-province'. To the commonly perceived and simplistic picture of the enclosure movement and its effects he brings a resounding dose of doubt, complexity and even some confusion. The confusion lies in the material, not in the manner in which it is treated. White airs the problems of the wide date range when enclosures took place and the prudent saving of money by owners agreeing to agree rather than to resort to legislation. It is also useful to see that not all large landowners were 'improvers' and that, for example, the Grosvenor and Arderne families allowed open field farming well into the eighteenth century. But what emerges strongly is the sheer complexity and variability of the subject. As White says 'we cannot be too deterministic in our analysis of the factors which prompted or delayed enclosure ...', but he demonstrates what factors were possible.

Introduction

Settlement Patterns

Mike Headon refreshingly addresses the problems of how we consider the definition of settlements and their shapes in north-east Wales. The names or labels that we give to features are, as he makes clear, very important: important because it shows what Headon calls 'a mode of thought', in this case the virtual ignoring of the problems of areas of dispersed settlement in favour of the easier problems of nucleated villages. There is also the whole problem of how contemporary people saw their own settlement, then how the settlement itself changed over time. Headon identifies nine classes of determiner and taken with his three types of known deliberately planned settlement within his study area produces a tentative taxonomy of fourteen classes with, in some cases, up to five sub-divisions. Again, this is work in progress and the next 'step', a small word for a huge task even for a representative sample, is to test these classes against the evidence to see what commonality might exist. This approach does challenge us to look at the evidence afresh.

Sharon Varey's paper on the farming economy of the parish of Baschurch is included within the settlement patterns theme but could equally well be placed elsewhere. For example while the main emphasis is on the farming economy of this area from 1550 to 2000, there is the important effect of transport on encouraging specialisation, by river for cheese, road to the wool markets of Oswestry and Shrewsbury and rail for milk. What causes pause for thought is the great variety of size of holding and type of agriculture which exists within an area of 8,000 acres, not to mention the changes that take place over 450 years. The way that farming economy is related to major building trends is very useful, especially the way in which this area contrasts with Shropshire generally. I have already referred to the problems of 'local' history, but surely the need for this level of scrutiny is shown by this paper. Otherwise the danger is that generalisations are made which do not bear much relation to what seems to have actually been happening.

Transport and Communications

Alan Crosby has described in detail the Cheshire Turnpikes in the landscape from 1700 up to – well he says 1850, but he gives us the intriguing thought that the motor age began only fifteen years after the final trusts were wound up. What if 'the demise of the trusts had been slower'? We would certainly have had different bodies to grumble at about routes in use today, made for horse drawn traffic with gentle gradients, but – for cars – lethally sharp corners. Beyond this Crosby claims that the landscape of Cheshire was changed in many ways by the work of the turnpike trusts and as his paper shows we have to agree. There is the acknowledged problem that by using the county boundaries we are cutting across routes, but there is still a large amount of material. The lessons to be learned are that a communications network can be built from scratch even in a landscape which has already been occupied for hundreds of years, that the infrastructure was not a sequential process and that in our area there really was an economic take-off in the 1770s and 1780s. Emerging from the conference venue at Ness one had a renewed interest and respect for the legacy of the many Wirral turnpike trusts.

Power

Tom Swailes introduces us to the early industrial landscape of Bollington. The stress is correctly on 'early'. There is a tendency to lump all aspects of industrial archaeology together. But Swailes shows how the evidence for the important early phases of the transformation of the industrial landscape can be teased out from under the nineteenth-century layers. While lines of transport form an important part in determining the present landscape, including a major change in axis, the story of the early phase is about power in the form of access to water. The supply of water was dependent upon what is called a 'generally modest' river which had to be augmented by the construction of reservoirs. My favourite piece is the way that the upstream mill could start work at 6 a.m. but it took two hours before the water could reach the lowest mill and work start there. However ground breaking the technology without a reliable source of power it is not much use, a lesson still true today.

Place-Names and Field-Names

One of the shorter contributions is from the CSLH Field-Names Research Group, facilitated by **Vanessa Greatorex**. This demonstrates the diversity of names present in the area, but also how they can be useful evidence of past economic activity or settlement, in some cases the only evidence from destroyed landscapes. It is worth noting that nearly half the conference papers make significant use of field- and place-names as evidence. For example Annakin-Smith has 'intakes' helping to define a possible core area of settlement, Headon has the hoary problem of 'hendre' and 'hafod', White has the wide variety of field-names derived from strip farming and the charming survival at 'Wally David' and Whittle has tenter fields supporting the fulling process. All these serve to show how this area of study and collection is an essential part of the work of a landscape historian and not to be denigrated, as I have heard it, as some form of 'stamp collecting' activity. This is not to say that the study of field-names does not have boring and disappointing moments.

Why does it matter?

At the end of the Conference I asked the question as to why local landscape history studies mattered? In producing a more considered answer first let us consider some recent comment. In an article published last year,[3] but based on a paper given in July 2009, David Dymond worried about the 'disdain of other kinds of historian' in judgement on the local historian – in whose company I think all attending the Conference would be proud to include themselves. In support of his argument Dymond quoted David Starkey as describing local history as 'a very limited thing'. But in his article Starkey is arguing for history to be part of the 'national story' and importantly, for me, 'it has to be about real people in real places'.[4] To be fair Starkey does worry about history losing sight of the big picture and cautions it could become 'a very limited thing – it becomes local history, it becomes regional history, it becomes racial history'. To refer back to Camden's *Britannia*, it is all of those things (yes, even racial history), and yet these pieces taken together formed a very influential 'bigger picture'. This is where the role of societies such as the Chester Society for Landscape History matters so much, because they can provide the academic and practical context and support to ensure that the role of specific studies in building the bigger picture is always remembered.

Amongst other matters that concerned Dymond were the relative roles in local history of 'professional' and 'non-professional' or 'amateur' or 'lay' historians. It is funny how there seem to be more categories for 'local' historian than other types of historian. However, listening to the papers given at the Conference and now published, it would be difficult to be sure (or whisper it, even concerned) about the relative status of any of the participants and authors. Instead there is a unity of interest, purpose and understanding which is as it should be.

As Camden's *Britannia* had a political purpose does a local landscape history society have a role in politics? As Dymond clearly states 'remembering that local historians are citizens with civic obligations, societies should not be afraid to lobby planners, councillors and MPs when threats appear and important issues are publicly debated. This is not easy, and frequently leads to disappointment, but the moral and educational obligations are clear and pressing on us all.'[5]

In practical terms 'the history of the landscape' had achieved official recognition in planning and agricultural policies.[6] Policies but unfortunately not legislation, which means that they are easier to change depending upon the political mood. A start was made in November 1990 with the promulgation of *Planning Policy Guidance; Archaeology and Planning* (PPG 16)[7] when the reasons for recognising the value of the physical remains of the past were set out and 'historic landscapes' made their first appearance. Under 'The Importance of Archaeology' it was stated:

4. Today's archaeological landscape is the product of human activity over thousands of years. ... It includes places of worship, defence installations, burial grounds, farms and fields, and sites of manufacture.

6. ... **They are part of our sense of national identity and are valuable both for their own sake and for their role in education, leisure and tourism** ...

14. ... **the key to the future of the great majority of archaeological sites and historic landscapes lies with local authorities** ... (Bold type emphasis as in the original.)

Four years later a planning guidance note (*Planning Policy Guidance, PPG 15, Planning and the Historic Environment*)[8] contained the following:

6.1 In its broadest sense, the historic environment embraces all those aspects of the country that reflect the shaping hand of human history ... our understanding of the historic environment now encompasses a much wider range of features, ... and also the value of historic townscape and landscape as a whole.

6.2 ... our understanding and appreciation of the historic environment now stretches beyond buildings to the spaces and semi-natural features which people have also moulded ... In the countryside, the detailed patterns of fields and farms, of hedgerows and walls, and of hamlets and villages, are among the most highly valued aspects of our environment.

I have set out some detail of PPGs 16 and 15 as they are now themselves history. Policies have changed and the new planning policy, anticipated at the conference, was published in March 2012. This is known as the *National Planning Policy Framework*.[9] In the Ministerial Foreword one of the aims of the changes is to get ordinary people and communities involved in the processes of change and the concept that 'historic landscape' is still there – 'our historic environment – buildings, landscapes, towns and villages'. In the glossary of definitions, part of the definition of 'Heritage Asset' is 'A ... landscape identified as having a degree of significance ... because of its heritage interest.' And in the midst of the historic environment policies, paragraph 170 recognises the need for appropriate 'assessment of historic landscape character' in drawing up Local Plans. All of which demonstrates not only the need to study, but to make the information publicly available and to be involved.

And finally

I was honoured to be asked to co-chair the Conference beside Graeme White. The fact that the conference papers are being published so rapidly reflects great credit on all concerned. The studies that are published in this volume are not just the products of ivory (or more suitably sandstone?) towers. There is the need for this work to define and assess for management and survival the complex inheritance that we are all stewards of today. We are inheritors of a long and honourable tradition of study. But the very last words on this, the 25th anniversary of the Chester Society for Landscape History, are those which infuse the final paper in this collection on Lifelong Learning, and sum up the atmosphere which pervaded the conference and represent the Society as a whole: **KNOWLEDGE** seasoned with **ENTHUSIASM!**

References

1. For a starting point in studying the *Britannia* see W.H. Herendeen, *William Camden: a Life in Context* (Woodbridge, 2007).
2. W.G. Hoskins, *Local History in England* (2nd edn, London, 1992).
3. D. Dymond, 'Does local history have a split personality?' in C. Dyer, A. Hopper, E. Lord and N. Tringham, *New Directions in Local History since Hoskins* (Hatfield, 2011), 13–28.
4. D. Starkey, 'The English historian's role and the place of history in English national life', *The Historian*, LXXI (Autumn 2001), 6–15.
5. D. Dymond, 'Does local history have a split personality?', 24.
6. A different approach has been used in Wales. Here, two volumes (1998 and 2001) of *Registered Landscapes of Outstanding Historic Interest* have been published by the Countryside Council for Wales and Cadw. They make the point that the defined areas are not the only historic landscapes of interest.

7. Department of the Environment, *Planning Policy Guidance, PPG 16, Archaeology and Planning* (November 1990).
8. Departments of the Environment and National Heritage, *Planning Policy Guidance, PPG 15, Planning and the Historic Environment* (September 1994).
9. <<http://communities.gov.uk/planningandbuilding/planningpolicy>> accessed 16/04/12.

1

STANLOW ABBEY: A TWENTY-FIRST CENTURY ASSESSMENT OF A TWELFTH-CENTURY CISTERCIAN MONASTERY

Stewart Ainsworth

Introduction

In 2010, an archaeological assessment of the site of Stanlow Abbey,[1] a Cistercian monastery and grange, was undertaken by English Heritage. This work focused on providing an informed analysis of the scheduled monument to underpin future management and conservation of the site.

The primary objective of the assessment was to acquire a rapid, up-to-date understanding of the remains to gauge the level of threat from the encroachment of woodland and general neglect within an industrial complex, much of which is now derelict. Permission for the assessment was restricted to a single day (10 August 2010), which imposed constraints both on the time available to inspect the site and the survey methodology that could be adopted. Due to the density of the woodland and the limited timescale, no measured survey was undertaken, but instead a rapid field inspection was conducted, followed by a desk-top assessment of readily available documentary and cartographic material, including examination of some primary sources at CALS.[2] Dense vegetation covers the majority of the site, and consequently airborne laser scanning or **lidar** (light direction and ranging) was used as a supplementary aid to help clarify some of the area, as this technique has been successfully applied in other heavily wooded landscapes.[3] This paper presents a summary of the results of the assessment.

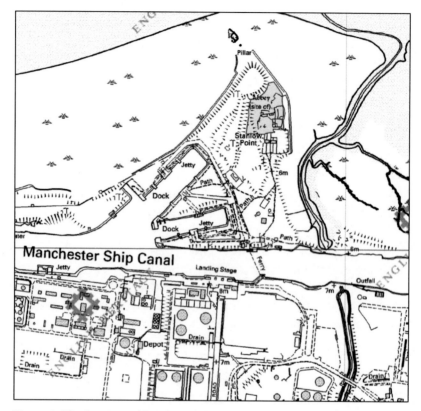

Figure 1. The location of Stanlow Abbey, reduced from the OS 1:10000 scale map. The grey shaded area shows the extent of the scheduled monument.

Location and landscape context (Figure 1)

The site of Stanlow Abbey is located on Stanlow Point, a low-lying Keuper Sandstone outcrop which juts out northwards into the Mersey estuary, immediately on the west side of the River Gowy. The 'Stan' element of Stanlow (OE – a stone or rock)[4] no doubt reflects the positioning of the abbey on an isolated rocky knoll standing on the edge of inhospitable tidal mudflats and marshes. It now falls within the northern part of an extensive oil refinery which borders the Mersey estuary. In the late nineteenth century, OS maps show that Stanlow Point was a coastal promontory projecting out into tidal mudflats, but it is now an 'island' having been physically separated from the main part of the landward refinery complex by the creation of the Manchester Ship Canal between 1887 and 1894. The landscape of Stanlow 'island' today comprises a mixture of industrial plant, buildings (many derelict), debris, large artificial earthen spoil mounds, dense undergrowth and tree cover. This 'island' is now isolated from the outside world, and despite the industrial setting, the sense of remoteness and austerity so favoured by the Cistercians for their choice of monastic sites still pervades. Ormerod, the Cheshire historian writing in 1816, conveyed the same sense of isolation that prevailed some seventy years before the onset of industrialisation: 'Even at the present day, it is difficult to select in Cheshire a scene of more comfortless desolation, than this cheerless marsh ...'.[5]

Modern-day studies of the remains

Only two surveys (with brief reports) have been made of the presumed abbey site: one in 1967 by Martin Roberts[6] (then a schoolboy), and one in 1985 by C. Williams and R. MacKinder.[7] Both are rudimentary, but the former is the more considered, and provides not only valuable information about the standing fabric and artefacts on the site when it was less covered in vegetation, but also offers a preliminary analysis of the overall site and its possible original layout (Figure 2). Unfortunately, both surveys are limited in scope and neither could be used to inform an up-to-date management prescription for the site. One archaeological watching brief was conducted in 2001 on the site of four houses during demolition, but this revealed very little as it took place outside the area where monastic

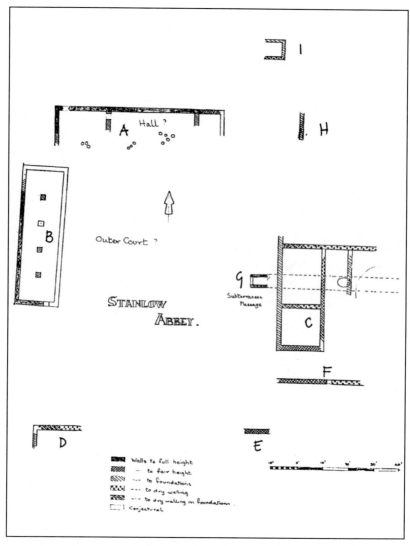

Figure 2. Survey of Stanlow Abbey undertaken by Roberts in 1967. The current assessment of this interpretation indicates that structures labelled A, B, D, E and G are likely to be part of the abbey and grange, the others being elements of the later farmstead on the site.

buildings or structures might be anticipated.[8] Stanlow Abbey was also the subject of a recent student dissertation although this adds little to the understanding of the layout of the site and no new field survey was conducted.[9]

Summary of the history of the site

The chartulary of Whalley Abbey known as the 'Coucher Book' contains numerous accounts and references to Stanlow but consultation and translation of this document was beyond the scope of the 2010 assessment. It is probable that further details of the history of the abbey may be contained in it to further illuminate the understanding of the site.[10] The following summary is based mostly on secondary sources, but it is sufficient to provide the background to the field assessment. The monastery at Stanlow was founded by John, sixth baron of Halton and constable of Chester. The founder's charter is dated 1178 although other chronicles suggest an earlier date of 1172, which may be when the first moves were initiated to establish Stanlow as a daughter house of Combermere Abbey.[11] Although the choice of location offered isolation, it was also vulnerable to the elements and the monastery suffered a number of catastrophes in the first hundred years or so after its foundation, which reflect its exposed location amongst the mudflats on the fringes of the windswept estuary. These included floods in 1279 and 1289, and in the intervening period the church tower collapsed during a storm in 1287. Also in 1289, a substantial part of the abbey was destroyed by fire. Representations were made to Pope Nicholas IV regarding the unsatisfactory nature of the site, suggesting that land on which the monastery stood was being worn away by the tides, and that the church and monastery buildings were being flooded to a depth of between 5 and 8 feet every year at the spring tide. The petition was later amended to state that only the offices which lay below the rock were being flooded to a depth of 3 to 5 feet.[12] On the face of it, the continued existence and viability of the site was at the mercy of the weather and tides, and the petitions were presented as a pragmatic response to environmental circumstance. In 1283, a licence was obtained to move to the new site at Whalley in Lancashire, and this move finally occurred in 1296.[13] However, that the move to Whalley was entirely driven by the forces of nature has been questioned, and other factors such as local competition for resources with the Abbey of St Werburgh and remoteness from the patron's developing interests in Lancashire may have been equally important.[14] The incumbent abbot resigned the abbacy, he and five monks remained at Stanlow, the new abbot and twenty monks moved to Whalley, and six others moved elsewhere.[15] After the move, Stanlow continued in use as a cell of Whalley Abbey until the Dissolution, during which time it maintained twelve monks[16] and appears to have become a grange of the new abbey, being listed as such in 1535.[17] The earliest account of the site, an inventory of 1537, provides a statement of the structures at Stanlow at the Dissolution: these structures are typically what might be expected of a grange, including a chapel, a garner [granary], servant's chamber, barn, madens [maiden's] chamber, buttery, kitchen, brewhouse, waynhouse [carthouse], hall and cowhouse.[18]

Following the Dissolution, a farm (probably the former grange) and lands at Stanlow came into the hands of Sir Richard Cotton, and subsequently (before c.1601), were sold to Sir John Poole, remaining with the Poole family until the early nineteenth century. After 1820, the farm and lands were sold to the Marquis of Westminster and thence to the Dean and Chapter of Chester.[19] The coming of the Manchester Ship Canal in 1887 undoubtedly signalled the demise of any remaining agricultural value of the Stanlow estate (approximately 230 acres of extra-parochial, tithe-free land)[20] and in 1922 the first of the oil docks was established on the 'island'. Throughout the remainder of the twentieth century there was a continuous expansion of the Shell oil installation on both sides of the canal, with further development of the oil docks in 1933, including the construction of a bitumen plant.[21] The 'island' has been in continuous industrial ownership and use ever since.

Descriptions of the site after the Dissolution

The first post-Dissolution description of the site (made in c.1601), albeit brief, suggests that by that date there was a farm in existence at Stanlow: 'Near unto Poole we see also Stanlow, now a farm of the said Mr Poole's'.[22] Again in 1656, there is reference to a farm at Stanlow belonging to Mr Pool[e],[23] whilst a further observation is made in a Disclaimer of 1681 by Sir James Poole in which mention is made of 'my house at Stanlowe'.[24] These sources would suggest that there was a farmstead at Stanlow during the first half of the seventeenth century. It is in this period that there is most likely to have been an adaptation (and possible demolition) of at least some of the structures identified in 1537, as well as the possible addition of others. There is no evidence from examination of later documentary and cartographic sources that there was any other substantial house or farmstead (other than that which can be identified today on the monastic site) anywhere else within the boundaries of Stanlow township with which those early observations might be confused, and therefore this points to continuity on the site of the earlier monastery and grange. The re-use of monastic buildings for farms and minor-gentry houses is well attested elsewhere and it seems likely that this was also the case at Stanlow.

Figure 3. Photograph of 'Farm and Site of Stanlow Abbey' published in *Perambulation of the Hundred of Wirral* by H.E. Young (1909).

From the mid-seventeenth century up to the mid-eighteenth century, little documentary evidence has been found relating to the site, although it seems probable that it continued in use as a farm (see below). Unfortunately, an engraving which has been alleged to show the remains of Stanlow Abbey preserved in a farmhouse in the early 1700s is of a different site.[25] This error has been caused by a misidentification of a Buck engraving of 1727 of the former grange at Ince Manor, about 2 kilometres to the east of Stanlow Point (confirmed by field inspection). It has been suggested by a nineteenth-century commentator, H.E. Young, that some farm buildings on the site at Stanlow were erected in about 1750.[26] A photograph of these[27] (as well as ground evidence) would support a mid-eighteenth-century date for the building of a substantial farmstead on the site (Figure 3).

It is possible that during this period of construction there may have been demolition of earlier structures or masking of earlier architecture within the later fabric. The scale of the farmhouse and the outbuildings in this photograph show that there had been a significant investment in this complex as a farm, presumably by the Poole family who owned it during the mid-eighteenth century. Throughout the latter part of the eighteenth century and into the early part of the nineteenth century, Land Tax returns between 1778 and 1832 indicate the existence of only one farm (and its land) occupied by a series of tenants within Stanlow township. It is presumably this farm which is shown on the first cartographic depiction of the site, Burdett's small-scale county map of 1777,[28] where 'Stanley house' is shown in approximately the correct position in relation to the River Gowy, and is also later depicted as 'Stanlow House' on a canal map of 1792.[29] The depiction of the farm on the 1777 county map in particular suggests that it at least had landscape prominence, and possibly an historical resonance, in what was otherwise mostly featureless marsh. Another small-scale county map, made in 1831,[30] shows a structure labelled 'House' in the same location as that shown for Stanlow House on the earlier maps of 1777 and 1792.

This is undoubtedly the same farm later described by Ormerod in 1816, and it is from him that we have the first identified association between the physical fabric of the farm at Stanlow and the monastic site.[31] It is from Ormerod's observations that all the later links between the farm and the monastery appear to have been derived. Ormerod notes the presence of 'a mean farm-house and barns, in which one or two ancient doorways [of the monastery] are preserved', and in the centre of the farmyard, a 'subterranean excavation' which was cut through rock, and headed eastwards under the buildings for 'about sixty yards' where it emerged on the verge of the River Gowy. Another similar underground feature is noted branching off at right angles to the north leading to a 'small, circular apartment' cut in the rock, from which bones and lead coffins had been revealed during a storm or tidal surge. Other features noted included carved fragments from buildings described as being from the remains of 'offices built below the rock on which the monastery stood', and the account further surmises that it is in this area where the flooding to a depth of 3 feet (as presented in the revised thirteenth-century petition) must have occurred. He also states that the rock which housed the monastery was 12 feet above the ordinary tide level.[32] However, apart from these few observations, it appears there was very little evidence at the time for extensive standing remains, or any clear indication of the site of the main conventual buildings.

There is an interesting, but unreferenced, contemporary description of Stanlow House at the time of the canal construction in 1887.[33] The 'original' (presumably c.1750)

Figure 4. Photographs of features as illustrated in *Perambulation of the Hundred of Wirral* by H.E. Young (1909). Both the doorway (now partially collapsed) and the 'subterranean passage' (monastic drain) still survive.

farmhouse is described as having its front door facing the river [north] with outbuildings to the back [south], and having subsequently been divided up into three sections (for three families) each with its own entrance and small garden and gate. Analysis of Young's early twentieth-century photograph noted above[34] indicates that it was taken from the south west, within the farm courtyard. It seems to corroborate the 1887 description, showing that the main farmhouse then was unequally divided into two on the south side, with individual entrances and low walled gardens, and outbuildings to the south. It seems probable that the north side was the original front of Stanlow House, facing out to the estuary. It is possible that the north front retained an entrance and that this could have formed the third division referred to. However, it is possible that a single-storey building adjoining the west side of the farmhouse may have had a domestic function, and that this could have alternatively been the third component. The photograph also indicates that the buildings were mostly built in brick. In Young's description, he notes 'four beautiful old circular columns which now support the roof of a cow-house', and an 'ancient doorway': he also included a photograph of the doorway and a subterranean passage,[35] which are undoubtedly the features noted by Ormerod (Figure 4). Young also refers to bones having been dug up from the gardens, with cartographic evidence indicating these gardens are likely to be to the east of the main outbuildings (see below).

OS map evidence: _c._1840–1898[36] (Figures 5 and 6)
From the late nineteenth century onwards the landscape of Stanlow Point is depicted on OS mapping, and can be seen to change from coastal, agricultural farmland containing the single isolated farmstead of Stanlow House, to a complex industrial landscape, physically separated from the 'mainland' by the

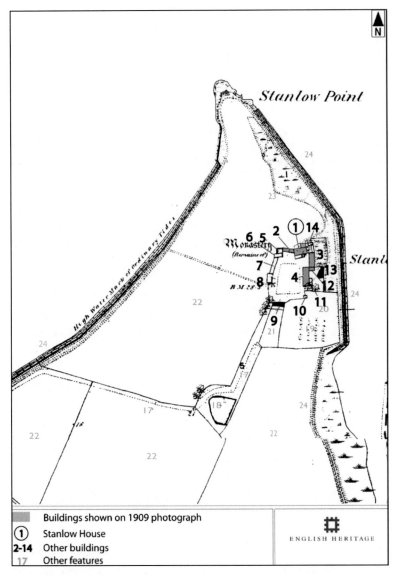

Figure 5. Reduced from the OS 25-inch scale map published in 1873 (surveyed in 1873).

construction of the Manchester Ship Canal (see below). The ending of the long continuity of occupation on the site seems to have been sometime after 1947 but before 1958, when the farm was described as having been abandoned.[37]

The earliest OS map which possibly links Stanlow House with the site of the abbey is the *c.*1840 1-inch scale map, where the general term 'Site of Abbey' is used, although the first map which firmly ties the remains of the abbey to the farm at Stanlow House is the 1873 25-inch scale map. This map shows a number of buildings arranged around a roughly rectangular court-yard measuring 65 metres by 50 metres, and some of the buildings and wall lines of the courtyard deviate from a true rectangular plan, particularly along the west and north sides. Both maps post-date Ormerod's work and it is probable that it was this information which was used as the authentication of the remains for the field surveyors. In particular, the nomenclature used on the 1873 map, 'Monastery (*Remains of)*', placed close to the depiction of the farm, indicated that some surviving medieval fabric had been interpreted by, or had been shown to the field surveyor within the farm for portrayal on the map. However, it is not immediately obvious on the map where this is.

The depiction of the north-west angle of Building 5,[38] (using 2 metre wide walls) is the convention used to show the ruins of what were considered to be structures of archaeological or historic interest on OS 25-inch scale County Series mapping; this cartographic tradition still continues to this day.[39] The very limited use of this convention there might indicate that in 1873 this walling was possibly the only part that was interpreted as being part of the monastic remains and worthy of depiction. This corner is still identifiable on the ground and is part of a longer section of what appears to be medieval sandstone walling (see Plate 2), and which contains an *in situ* doorway.

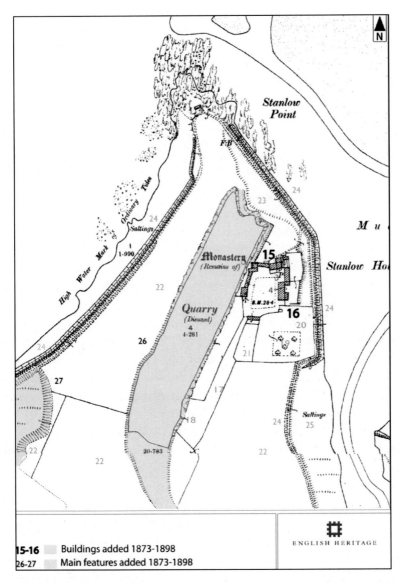

Figure 6. Reduced from the OS 25-inch scale map published in 1898 (revised in 1897).

This is also the doorway which appears in the photograph in Young's 1909 publication. Between the 1873 and 1898 map editions, there are a few minor changes to the layout of the buildings. A structure to the east of Building 4 (Building 13) was demolished, a small outshut was added to Building 2 (Building 15) and a small, detached unroofed structure (Building 16) was added. From the small size of the yards, it is possible that Building 14 may have comprised a series of small animal pens and possible privy block.

It is also not clear from the map alone which is Stanlow House (the farmhouse built *c.*1750 and still extant in the photograph of *c.*1909), but it can be confidently identified as the rectangular structure at the east end of the north range (Building 1): it is aligned almost east-west and measures about 15 metres by 7 metres. Its alignment is slightly at odds with the other buildings suggesting that it may have been imposed on an earlier layout. The photograph also shows the relative positions of a number of other buildings which can be equated with the layout on the 1873 and the 1898 25-inch scale maps. Stanlow House is clear as the central feature in the photograph as a (then) two-storey structure with two doorways along the south façade and a small walled garden in front. To the left (west), and abutting the gable end of the farmhouse, is a narrower, single-storey structure (Building 2). To the right (east) of the farmhouse, and offset approximately at right-angles to it, is a two-storey barn which is partly unroofed at that time (Building 3); further to the right (south east), but partly in front of Building 3, is a two-storey, brick barn with a line of ventilation slits along the western façade of the upper storey (Building 4). The majority of the building fabric appears to be brick. There is no obvious indication of any monastic architecture on the structures on the photograph. The small size of other roofed structures depicted on the 1873 map (Buildings 5–14) suggests that they are mostly outbuildings.

Other aspects of the landscape at this time can be interpreted from the 1873 map. Immediately to the east of Stanlow House, the depiction of the narrow paths and lines of shrubs indicates a garden enclosure. Approaching the courtyard from the south is what appears to be a lane (17) indicating that the entrance was at the south-west corner, and along this lane is a pond (18). Other peripheral features include an orchard (19), and enclosures (20–21). To the west, north and south of the farmstead the map indicates a series of fields (22), and to the north east, what appears to be the former coastline is indicated by an irregular line of hachures (23), immediately west of a what is clearly a flood bank with stone-revetment, which is also shown around the west side of Stanlow Point (24). This continues as an earthen flood bank at the south east. Seaward of the flood bank, the flats are shown as being used as Saltings in 1898 (25). This major flood defence, shown on the 1873 map, clearly pre-dates the creation of the Manchester Ship Canal, which was not started until 1887. Given that this flood bank was not mentioned by Ormerod in relation to the outfall of the 'subterranean excavations', it is possible that it was constructed after 1816, but possibly before c.1840, as its presence can be inferred on the OS 1-inch scale map of that date.[40] It is possible that some material for the flood bank may have been excavated from the former coastal slope immediately to the west. However, whatever the date of construction of the elaborate flood defences, the most likely context would be the protection of the farm at Stanlow House and the farmland around.

Whilst only minor changes to the farm area are evidenced between the map editions of 1873 and 1898, major changes are obvious immediately to the west. There, a large rectangular strip of ground (approximately 360 metres by 60 metres) on a north-east to south-west orientation bordering the western side of the courtyard, had been dug out as a quarry (26). On the 1898 map (surveyed 1897) the quarry is clearly by then redundant as it is termed 'Disused'. The depiction of a hard line within this quarry area implies that it contained water over the majority of its length at this stage, and this seems to be confirmed by Young's photograph of the doorway,[41] where water can be seen in the quarry in the background. The digging of this quarry for stone and earth for the embankments of the Ship Canal is reported in a near contemporary source by E.W. Cox in 1892.[42] Importantly, Cox describes how the quarry cut across an 'ancient graveyard' revealing large quantities of bones and skeletons, and 'finely-cut, moulded stones', including fragments of a doorway, with a double tier of shafts on each side (surmised by Cox to be the western door of the abbey). Cox also notes that a few shafts of round pillars had been re-used in the farm buildings (possibly the ones noted by Young) and that other architectural fragments, including window jambs and arches, pillar base, and fragments of chapel arcade and cloisters were found. He also notes that the walls of the abbey had been 'grubbed up to the very foundations' suggesting that some wall lines were traceable as robber trenches, etc. The area of the quarry to which the accounts refer (but which is not stated in the original account) is likely to be at the very northern end (see below).

In the period covered by this mapping the 'island' became physically separated by the construction of the Manchester Ship Canal. This major feature clearly impacted on the overall field patterns around, and although the boundaries of the lane at the south (17) were still extant, the digging of the quarry and canal had now clearly made access along this route from the south west redundant, and the pond (18) had disappeared.

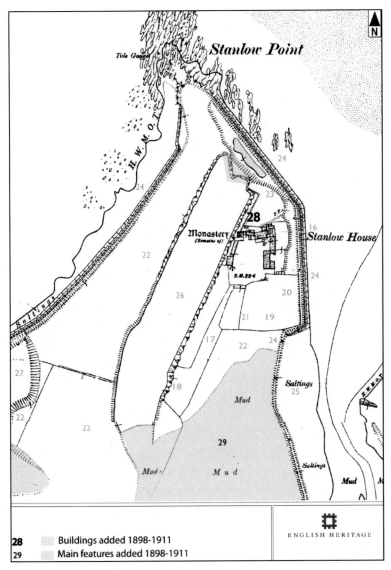

Figure 7. Reduced from the OS 25-inch scale map published in 1911 (revised in 1908).

OS map evidence: c.1898–1911[43] (Figure 7)

Between the dates of the 1898 and 1911 map editions, little change is indicated in the immediate vicinity of Stanlow House, apart from the addition of one small building and boundary (28) north of the north range of the courtyard. Buildings 5 and 6 were by 1908 un-roofed, the former showing very small rectangular structures had been added, or had been revealed when the internal areas were exposed. It is possible that by 1908 the farm at Stanlow House had started to go into decline due to its isolation caused by the canal, as Young notes in 1909 that it was falling into decay and was occupied only by a fisherman and a wild-fowler.[44] The orchard (19) was no longer shown on the later revision. The major change in this period is at the south, where a large area to the west of the earthen flood bank (24) is shown as 'Mud' (29). The dashed line depicting its boundary continues to the south-east corner of the flooded area within the former quarry (26) and implies water and wet ground over a large area in 1908. The earlier mapping suggests that this was formerly fields, possibly having earlier been reclaimed for agriculture by the erection of the flood bank prior to 1873, but reversion to mud suggests a susceptibility to flooding in this area.

OS map evidence: c.1911–1959[45] (Figures 8–10)

This is the period within which most changes to the 'island' area occur and a number of maps cover this period. From the map evidence it can be confidently interpreted that there had been four main additions to the landscape which are relevant to this assessment during the period from 1911 up to 1938; the docks to the south west (30), the spread of the industrial complex including part infill of the former quarry, a large building north of No. 1 dock (31), and a building (32)

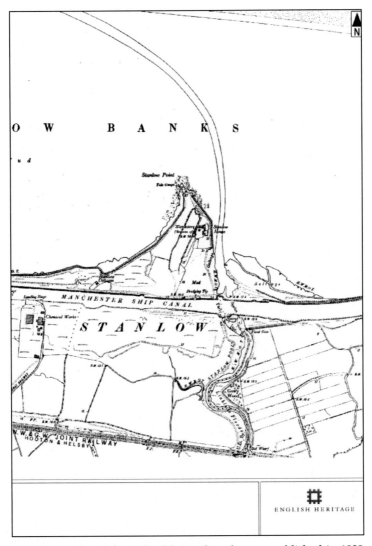

Figure 8. Reduced from the OS 6-inch scale map published in 1929 (revision date not established). The southern of the two docks at Stanlow was built in 1922, and as this is not shown on this 1929 map it is likely to have been revised before 1922.

immediately south of the farmstead at Stanlow House. All had seemingly been either constructed or were in the process of construction between those two dates. By the date of the 6-inch scale Provisional Edition of 1954 (which was revised for changes up to 1949), the buildings on the east and west ranges of the farmstead courtyard (Buildings 3, 4, 11, 12, 7, 8, 9, 10) and also Building 32, had apparently been demolished. The implication is that this had happened between 1938 and 1949, although the later map and field evidence shows this was clearly not the case. The 1954 map exhibits a number of other inconsistencies which cast doubt on its reliability. Aerial photographs taken in 1947 show that four semi-detached houses had been built south of the farm,[46] and these are likely to be what was shown schematically on the 1938 map as one building (Building 32). The two western houses (33–34) had long gardens extending for about 28 metres south and 20 metres north bordering on to the former southern boundary of the farm courtyard. The eastern pair of houses (35–36) had shorter rear gardens which only extend for about 8 metres north of the buildings. The houses and gardens had been inserted into the western half of the former orchard enclosure (20). Access to the houses was via a split footpath which approached from the south. The 1947 air photograph shows that the remainder of this enclosure contained rows of what appear to be orchard trees and this area was still defined as an orchard on the detailed OS 50-inch scale mapping surveyed in 1958. Building 31 on the 1938 map is the 'Club' on the 1959 OS map.

By 1947, the air photographs show that the quarry to the west (26) had been filled in and that the boundaries of the lane (17) and western boundary of enclosure (21) had been removed. It is not clear whether all of the extensive area of

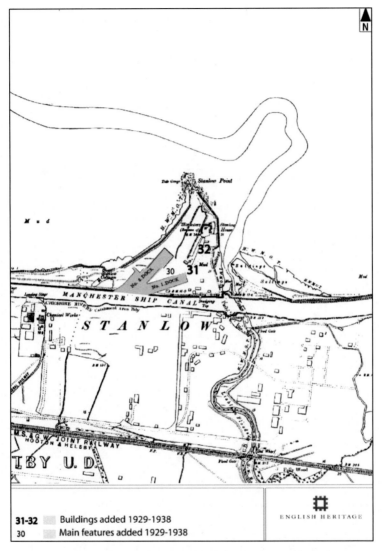

Figure 9. Reduced from the OS 6-inch scale map published in 1938 (revision date not established). This edition may not have been fully revised during the emergency mapping programme prior to World War Two.

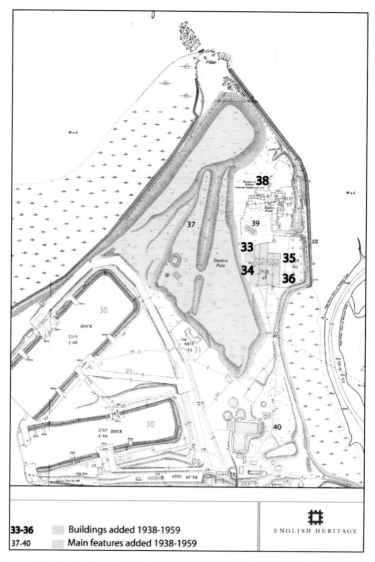

Figure 10. Reduced from the OS 25-inch scale map derived from 50-inch scale: published 1959, surveyed 1958.

artificial plateau-like mounds shown on the 1959 map had been constructed by then, but most are likely to have been. A number of structures in this area which are shown on the 1959 map are also not visible in 1947, suggesting a continuous process of change. These large mounds (37), which dominate the landscape today, cover an area of about 3.5 hectares, and are probably the waste from digging of the dock basins in the early twentieth century (30). Whatever their date of construction (and their layout would suggest that there is more than one phase) the mounds clearly overlie a large tract at the northern end of the 'island', including most of the former quarry (26), most of the area of the former lane (17), and western part of enclosure (21), although the original entrance to the courtyard was not masked by this dumping. Between 1908 and 1958 there was an expansion of what appears to be small-scale paddocks and a new, small building or shed (Building 38) immediately to the north of Stanlow House, although the impact of changes in this area seems minimal.

Because of the larger scale of survey of the 1959 map (1:1250 survey undertaken in March 1958) as opposed to 1:2500 scale of earlier mapping, the farm complex is depicted in more detail, with much of the layout as shown on the 1873 edition still identifiable. In 1958, of the buildings visible on the c.1909 photograph, Stanlow House and the structures to the west (Buildings 1 and 2) were still shown as being roofed; the barn to the east (Building 3) is shown in outline as unroofed with smaller structures within it; the barn (Building 4) was also shown in outline as unroofed, as was Building 11 to the rear of it. Buildings 12, 10, 14 along the east range are roofed at this date, as is Building 5. This map also confirms that by 1958 the entrance to the courtyard and site generally, had moved to the south-east corner. At the west, the former western perimeter of the range (and rear of Buildings 7 and 8) can be identified, and although Building 8 had been demolished, the internal divisions of Building 7 are shown. Similarly, at the south, the courtyard boundary is identifiable but Building 9 had been demolished. A mound is shown in the courtyard at the south west and this may well have been formed from demolition debris from the buildings (39). At this stage some structures are termed 'Ruin', and it seems that a state of dereliction prevailed at the farm. During the latter part of the twentieth century numerous industrial structures have been constructed on the fringes of the assessment area (e.g. 40) but these have had no impact on the monastic site.

OS map evidence: _c._1959–2010[47]

The analysis of the decline towards the tree-covered landscape of Stanlow Point today has been mostly undertaken using aerial photographs taken between 1971 and 2000, as post-1959 editions of the 50-inch scale maps could not be traced. In 1971, aerial photographs show that most of the original farmstead area was in the process of becoming overgrown with scrub and trees, although the four semi-detached houses appear to have been occupied, as the gardens were still tended. Also, a number of the industrial structures shown on the 1959 50-inch scale map east of the southern dock had been removed. This was much the same picture in 1985 when the area was photographed again, although by this time the scrub and tree cover is denser and had encroached more to the south. The structures and area around the docks to the south would appear to be still maintained at this date. Aerial photographs taken in 1999 show that by this date the gardens of the semi-detached houses were also overgrown, indicating that the houses had been abandoned. By this point scrub and tree cover had become denser across most of the 'island', and it appears that the area around the industrial structures east of the dock was by then showing signs of neglect.

The current OS digital Mastermap (digitised from the 1959 50-inch scale mapping but with undated revision – see Plate 1) still shows the four semi-detached houses despite the fact that they were demolished in 2001 under supervision of an archaeological watching brief.[48] The houses were only demolished to the level of the damp-proof course and a small rockery was removed. No below-ground excavation was conducted, and all the material from the demolition was dragged to the south of the site of the houses. No features of any archaeological significance were revealed; some fragments of sandstone blocks of possible medieval and post-medieval origin were recorded although none had any decorative features to aid dating. The modern digital map retains the footprint of many of the parts of buildings and boundaries of the former farmstead shown on maps from 1873 to 1959, although many walls which exist on the ground are not shown.

Results of the assessment (Plate 1)

The majority of the plan-form of the various buildings on the site shown on maps from 1873–2010 survives as low walling (much of which is covered by dumps of collapsed material and vegetation), including some stretches of possible medieval date. The footprint of Stanlow House itself (Building 1) is easily identifiable by low brick walls with dressed-stone footings in places, as are the remains of Buildings 2, 3, 4, 6, 9, 10, 11, 14 and 15, along with a number of other outbuildings and garden walls which are shown on the detailed 1959 OS map. Many brick-built wall lines also evidence internal features within the farm buildings, and also a number of features exist which are not shown on the map.

The site contains a wealth of abandoned cultural material on the surface (such as pottery and artefacts) associated with the occupation of Stanlow House, as well as farmyard debris and architectural fabric such as elaborate wrought-iron window frames. This would imply that despite the large-scale industrial impacts elsewhere on the 'island' this area has survived relatively intact since the late 1950s and because of its isolation has not been heavily disturbed since then. Surprisingly, only minor disturbance seems to have been caused by industrial activity, mainly evidenced by a small amount of rusting pipe-work, a few groundworks and an underground chamber at the south west of the courtyard.

Only three sections of early, probable medieval, sandstone walling were identified amongst the demolished buildings. These can be correlated with walls which originally formed the north sides of Buildings 2 and 5, the west and south sides of Building 7, and an underground stone-lined drain with a probable original entry culvert. Both of the above-ground medieval walls have been part of the farm outbuildings shown on mapping since 1873 through to 1959. These sections of wall are reasonably well-preserved, but it has not been possible to firmly establish their context as part of the original abbey or later grange.

The first section of probable medieval wall (Plate 2), which was incorporated into the rear of Buildings 2 and 5, runs approximately east to west, is about 15 to 20 metres in length and stands to a height of 1.5 metres, with a change of direction along its length (Roberts's building A – which he interpreted as a hall). A short section of similar walling at the west returns at right-angles to the south and appears to be the gable-end. At the north-west corner of this building, a doorway is *in situ* along the north wall. This doorway incorporates chamfered jambs and lintels (now partly collapsed), and appears to have

Figure 11. The southern gable of Building 7. This structure may have originally been within the monastic outer court, and subsequently incorporated into the grange and post-Dissolution farm buildings.

been altered over time. A mason's mark has been previously noted on the right-hand jamb of the doorway.[49] This doorway was the one photographed from the north in *c.*1909, and there has clearly been loss to the height of the wall and changes to the doorway since that date. There has also been some patching and repair which appears relatively modern. There is another blocked doorway further east along this wall, which also shows many periods of repair, and possibly even rebuild. Two possible walls, which may be the remains of original internal building divisions, were noted projecting from this wall although without clearing of vegetation this interpretation is somewhat tentative (similar features were shown on Roberts's survey). To the south, a section of a round stone column is visible but does not appear to be *in situ*. This seems likely to be a part of one of the columns noted by Young in 1909 and Roberts in 1967. One

Figure 12. The western end of the main monastic drain photographed from approximately the same point as the view illustrated in Figure 4.

other decorated stone, possibly a section of window tracery, was also noted in this area.

The second section of probable medieval walling originally formed the western side of the courtyard on the 1873 map and the rear of Building 7. This also exhibits numerous periods of repairs where the fabric is visible (Roberts's building B). Some sections stand to an impressive height of between 2.5 and 3 metres, and the amount of collapse around the walls at the south west implies that these were originally of substantial build. A return at the south is possibly a gable-end wall (Figure 11). The plinths shown on Roberts's plan were not visible in the undergrowth. To the west of Buildings 5 and 7 there are large earthworks which define the former limits of the quarry and the later waste heaps. The area of the courtyard to the east of Building 7 has been platformed into the natural slope and may be part of the original abbey topography. This cutting/levelling may have originally provided shelter from prevailing winds from the west and may have also performed the dual function of an original quarry for the abbey building stone.

Towards the eastern side of the former farm courtyard, the third section of medieval sandstone walling comprises a section of an underground, 1.5 metres wide, stone-lined drain, heading off to under the remains of Building 4, which is immediately to the east. Only the first few metres are visible (the rest is buried), but the scale and architecture of its construction suggests that this is the original main drain of the monastery (Figure 12). There has been some partial collapse of the entrance to the drain and it appears to be much in the same state as when photographed in *c.*1909. It seems highly probable that this is the 'subterranean passage' first observed by Ormerod and subsequently reported by others. Ormerod stated in 1816 that it emerged 60 yards to the east, but this would have taken it out beyond the line of the present flood bank, thereby supporting the suggestion that this flood defence may have been erected after that date; if so it seems probable that some of it may have been destroyed during the construction work.

There are other areas where there is a suggestion of some medieval stonework at ground level, although these are only visible between the piles of collapsed brick walling and brambles: only small sections were observed and so the identification is tentative. At the south end of Building 3 are a few, roughly-fashioned, ground-fast stones showing through the turf where it has been disturbed. Young's photograph of the drain shows that Buildings 3 and 4 were originally built mostly in brick with dressed-stone base-courses. This is confirmed by the remains, which are easy to identify on the ground, and the build seems to be consistent with an eighteenth-century date. Neither building contains any obvious original or re-used medieval stone in the surviving footprint. Therefore, these few, crudely-dressed stones may be part of an earlier structure. Around the south-west, south, and south-east perimeter of the courtyard, other short sections of low, possible *in situ* medieval walling are visible, although this boundary has had many later additions and is heavily covered in undergrowth, making interpretation difficult. One of the sections at the south west is where the original entrance to the courtyard is likely to have been (at the end of the lane shown on the 1873 map), and where possibly an original monastic gatehouse might be expected. Some possible medieval stonework has been re-used on the flood defences, although the majority of the revetment consists of purposely-cut stone. A number of other structures shown on Roberts's plan (and on that by Williams and MacKinder) can be identified as farmstead remains rather than having monastic origins.

No structures were obvious immediately to the north of the remains of Stanlow House, where there is a small area of high ground with no evidence of having been disturbed by later land-use. This is the eastern part of the area that was sliced through by the nineteenth-century quarrying and where remains suggestive of a church and cloister were found and reported in 1892. This is one of the few areas (the others being the former gardens to the east of Buildings 3 and 4, and the courtyard area of the farm) where there have been no significant identifiable farm buildings or industrial activity, and this area therefore may have high archaeological potential for the below-ground preservation of part of the abbey church. During the assessment, some sandstone blocks were glimpsed in the undergrowth of this area, both loose and embedded in the ground; a slight earthwork mounding was also observed in gaps in the bushes (these are confirmed by a series of features evident on the lidar). It is possible that these may simply be garden paths and the remains of sheds visible on the 1947 aerial photographs, although this could not be confirmed due to the vegetation.

Evaluation of the monastic layout

Because so little survives above ground of the medieval monastery and grange, interpretation of the original layout of both has to remain somewhat speculative. The most diagnostic surviving monastic feature on the site is the drain, and although this may provide at least some positional reference on a north-south axis in relation to the site of a reredorter, an east-west placement of structures using this is less secure. The few sections of standing masonry provide no clear indication of their context due to the current obscured state, and therefore this assessment can only attempt to evaluate the validity of the overall understanding that existed prior to this new appraisal. This understanding has been based mostly on Ormerod's observations (subsequently repeated in derivative publications by others), and Roberts's interpretation, which place the abbey church on the higher ground, i.e. north of the remains of Stanlow House. These hypotheses have not been re-evaluated until now.

In reality, very little is known of the layout and size of Stanlow Abbey. It seems likely that the layout at Stanlow would follow a standard Cistercian plan for a small, late twelfth-century monastery with the church to the north of the cloister, and a standard arrangement of conventual buildings.[50] It has also been suggested that the west range (lay brothers' dormitory) and church may have been of the same size as at Whalley Abbey.[51] In addition, as the number of monks had been significantly reduced by the end of the thirteenth century, it would seem unlikely that the main conventual buildings would have increased in size and complexity (if they survived at all), as they did at many other monasteries which lasted to the Dissolution. If the layouts of three local Cistercian sites at Whalley Abbey, Valle Crucis, and Sawley Abbey are used for comparison (all these monasteries follow a reasonably standard plan although they had a significantly longer lifespan and complexity of change), it can be seen that all have cloisters of about 30 to 40 metres square, with the lay brothers' dormitory along the west range, church to the north, kitchens and refectory along the south range, chapter house, sacristy and monks' dormitory along the east range, with the latter buildings having a reredorter at their southern end. Whalley Abbey in particular may provide the closest comparator because of the direct transference of monks and influence from Stanlow. By using a maximum figure of about 40 metres square for the cloister and a monks' dormitory of about 30 metres length as a template, and overlaying a simple, putative plan based on this in relation to the entrance to the drain at Stanlow (which should be close to the south end of the monks' dormitory), then this would place the southern range of the main cloister close to the rear of Buildings 2 and 5. That a roughly east-west wall of probable medieval build exists here (where one might be anticipated) may support this interpretation, although this in itself is not conclusive.

The architectural finds observed during the cutting of the quarry in 1892 seem to suggest, but not with absolute certainty, a cloister and church. Whilst there is no precise indication of the site of these finds, it is the area to the north and west of Building 5 where the impact of the quarrying recorded in 1892 comes closest to the standing remains, within which medieval walling had earlier been identified by Ormerod. The 1898 OS map clearly shows that the western buildings of the farm formed the boundary of the quarrying and that this did not impact on the farm itself. Taken together, the little evidence there is would suggest that the finds suggestive of a cloister and church would have been encountered in the northern part of the quarry. In this postulated layout therefore, the stone walls observed at the rear of Buildings 2 and 5 could indeed be part of the range to the south of the cloister, possibly the kitchen or refectory as Roberts suggests (and later incorporated into the grange). At Whalley Abbey, the kitchen and refectory are arranged in a linear fashion along the south range, and it is possible the same arrangement existed at Stanlow.

The wall at the rear of Building 7 (Roberts's building B) is markedly off an east-west/north-south axis and therefore is likely to have been outside the main conventual area, for instance in an outer court, where it is less likely to have been constrained by the requirement for Cistercian architectural rigour. This further supports the placement of the church to the north. If this interpretation is correct, the remains of Stanlow House would be located approximately over the south-east corner of the cloister, and extend into the range containing the monks' dormitory. Buildings 3 and 4 would also lie close to the line of the monks' dormitory, and on a general north-south axis, with the west wall of Building 3 possibly being close to the line of the east wall of the monk's dormitory. Although this plan is tentative, it is interesting to note how the later farm buildings here maintain the linearity and axis that might be expected for the monks' dormitory range.

In this layout, an overall comparative measurement for the abbey church of anywhere between about 55 to 70 metres east-west might be anticipated. If this reconstruction is correct then the area of relatively undisturbed ground north of Stanlow House would be where the transepts, east end of the church, most of the east range of the cloister, including the chapter-house, and part of the south range of the cloister would have been located. However, most of the nave and west range would have been lost to the quarrying, and possibly some of the east end may have been subject to coastal erosion. It is possible that the relatively undisturbed gardens to the east of Buildings 3 and 4 might preserve the remains of an infirmary and cemetery, which might account for the finds of lead coffins and bones along this eastern fringe. Ormerod's description of a 'small circular apartment' somewhere along this seaward side perhaps suggests the site of a rock-cut crypt.

In this layout, the position and alignment of the main drain, as well as servicing a reredorter, is ideally placed to serve an outer courtyard with kitchens and refectory along its north side, as drainage here is favoured towards the south and east by the natural topography. Also, if an infirmary was located to the east of Stanlow House (in the garden area formerly occupied by Building 13) then drainage from there would also naturally feed into the same drain and it is possible that Ormerod's account of another 'subterranean passage' here may be another drain.

The longevity of the plan-footprint of the farm and courtyard suggest that this is largely a fossilisation of the original outer monastic courtyard, service buildings, and possibly some of the remnants of conventual buildings to the south and possibly east of the main cloister. As a unit, it seems plausible that this could be the complex which was retained as the monastic cell/grange in the late thirteenth century and which continued in use to the Dissolution, with the structures listed in 1537 possibly arranged around this courtyard. The positioning and odd alignment of service buildings (e.g. Buildings 7 and 8) outside the main conventual area is likely to have been governed by the availability of solid ground in what was otherwise likely to be floodable marshland, with the most favourable, higher ground being retained for the construction of the abbey church. The lidar modelling demonstrates that the area to the north of the site of Stanlow House is indeed the highest surviving part of what is likely to be original 'monastic' ground surface, and that the farm courtyard (and original outer court) is the lowest (Plate 3). Only a small area of slightly higher ground than the courtyard separates it from the old coastline at the south-east corner and this would make the original outer court (and any buildings around it such as the kitchens, refectory, monks' day room and warming room, as well as outer court buildings) the most susceptible area to storm and tidal surges prior to the insertion of flood banks. The lidar model shows that of the known surviving monastic area, it is only likely to be the courtyard and buildings immediately around it that would be prone to flooding during tidal or storm surge. It is entirely possible that this may be the area referred to in the thirteenth-century petition to Pope Nicholas IV as the 'offices' which were being flooded to a depth of 3 to 5 feet, and it may be the case that the main drain itself may have acted as an unwelcome conduit for floodwater ingression into the courtyard.

Summary
In essence, this current assessment would largely support both Ormerod's and Roberts's overall hypotheses. However, allocating functions to the few surviving building remains within the context of the 1537 inventory was not possible under the prevailing site conditions and the limited timescale available. Due to the major landscape changes resulting from quarrying and the subsequent creation of enormous waste mounds it is unlikely that there will be any survival of early monastic structures to the west and north-west of the Buildings 5, 7 and 8. This would include the loss of the lay brothers' dormitories, the western part of the cloister, and most of the nave. It is clear from the known history that to view the original site of the monastery as having been 'abandoned' at

any point in its pre-Dissolution history is potentially misleading – it appears to have simply changed in scale and function. The same remains true of the post-Dissolution period, where there is evidence of a continuation of occupation and farming activity on the site through to the mid-twentieth century. Although the site had a monastic function in one form or another for about 360 years, it seems to have had a longer life (around 420 years) as an entirely secular residence and farmstead. It is important that this domestic and agricultural continuity is weaved into the current understanding of the site, and that the archaeological impact and architectural value of this, as well as the development and impact of the industrial landscape, informs the management and conservation of the site for the future.

References

1. Throughout this paper the modern spelling of Stanlow (which has been used by map-makers since the nineteenth century) is used, although historically it has been spelt as Stanlawe, Stanlaw, Stanlow, Stanlowe and at one point Stanley in the various reference sources consulted.
2. English Heritage Level 2 survey as defined in S. Ainsworth, M. Bowden and D. McOmish, *Understanding the Archaeology of Landscapes: a Guide to Good Recording Practice* (Swindon, 2007).
3. S. Crutchley and P. Crow, *The Light Fantastic: Using Airborne Lidar in Archaeological Survey* (Swindon, 2009).
4. J. McN. Dodgson, *The Place-Names of Cheshire*, V (Cambridge, 1981), 350.
5. G. Ormerod, *The History of the County Palatine and City of Chester* [hereafter *History of Cheshire*], II (2nd edn, London, 1882), 398.

6. M. Roberts, 'Survey of Stanlow Abbey' (1967, unpubl. report deposited in Cheshire HER).
7. C. Williams and R. MacKinder, 'Stanlow Abbey' *Liverpool University Archaeology Newsletter* (issue 2 1986); C. Williams and R. MacKinder, 'Draft survey report on Stanlow Abbey' (1985, unpubl. report deposited in Cheshire HER).
8. C.J. Crowe, 'Numbers 1-4 Stanlow Point, Stanlow Island, Ellesmere Port, Cheshire' (AAA Archaeological Advisors unpubl. report, 2002).
9. R. Parkinson, 'Why was the Cistercian Abbey of Stanlow abandoned? Will of God or Human Weakness?' (University of Chester unpubl. BA dissertation, 2009).
10. See *VCH Lancs*, II, 131–39, fn. 253. The chartulary was edited in four volumes for the Chetham Society by W.A. Hulton, 'The Coucher Book or Chartulary of Whalley Abbey' volume I, *Chetham Society*, 1st ser., X (1847), 1–338; volume II, 1st ser. XI (1847), 339–636; volume III, 1st ser. XVI (1848), 637–936; volume IV, 1st ser. XX (1849), 937–1314. See also C.D. King, 'The Whalley Coucher Book and the dialectical phonology of Lancashire and Cheshire 1175–1350' (University of St Andrews unpubl. PhD thesis, 1991).
11. *VCH Lancs*, II, 131; *VCH Ches*, III, 152.
12. *VCH Lancs*, II, 131–39; Ormerod, *History of Cheshire*, II, 399.
13. *VCH Lancs*, II, 131–39.
14. S. Matthews, 'Cheshire's failed religious houses', *Ches.Hist.*, XLII (2002–03), 43–44.
15. Ormerod, *History of Cheshire*, II, 399.
16. Ormerod, *History of Cheshire*, II, 399.
17. D. Knowles and R.N. Hadcock, *Medieval Religious Houses: England and Wales* (London, 1971), 132.
18. M.E.C. Walcott, 'Inventory of Stanlow', *THSLC*, new ser. XII (1872), 53–56.

19. Ormerod, *History of Cheshire*, II, 399–400; Land Tax Returns 1778–1832: CALS: QDV 2/394; P. Sulley, *The Hundred of Wirral* (Birkenhead, 1889), 164; W.W. Mortimer, *The History of the Hundred of Wirral* (first published 1847, republished Manchester, 1972), 261.
20. Ormerod, *History of Cheshire*, II, 400.
21. Shell Petroleum Company Limited, *Britain's New Industry: Stanlow 1949* (London, 1949), 9–19.
22. *Webb's Itinerary* (c.1601) quoted in Walcott, 'Inventory of Stanlow', 53.
23. D. King, *The Vale Royal of England* (1656, abridged reprint by T. Hughes, London, 1852), 116.
24. Disclaimer by Sir James Poole of Poole: CALS: EEC/33608.
25. Engraving of c.1730 by J. Strutt in C. Hulbert, *Cheshire Antiquities* (1838), plate opposite p. 45; misidentification repeated in Crowe, 'Numbers 1–4 Stanlow Point', Section 2.2 and reproduced as Figure 4 in that report, citing Hulbert.
26. H.E. Young, *Perambulation of the Hundred of Wirral* (Liverpool, 1909), 72–73.
27. Young, *Perambulation of the Hundred of Wirral*, plate facing p. 66.
28. P.P. Burdett, *Survey of the County Palatine of Chester* (1777). Scale: five and seven eighths inches equals six miles.
29. J. Turner, T. Morris, J. Chamberlaine and W. Cawley, *Wirral Canal and Branch to Trafford* (1792): CALS: QDP3. Scale not given.
30. Bryant, *Map* (1831). Scale: one inch and a quarter to one statute mile.
31. Ormerod, *History of Cheshire*, II, 398–400.
32. Ormerod, *History of Cheshire*, II, 400 fn. b.

33. L.G. Lynch, *The Changing Face of Ellesmere Port* (Chester, nd), 112: CALS: P/ELLE/L.

34. Young, *Perambulation of the Hundred of Wirral*, plate facing p. 66.

35. Young, *Perambulation of the Hundred of Wirral*, 66–73 and plate facing p. 71.

36. OS 1-inch scale first edition map surveyed *c*.1840 (David and Charles reprint, 1970); OS 1:2500 scale (County Series First Edition) Cheshire (Western Division) Sheet XXIII. 16. Surveyed 1873 (Published 1873); OS 1:2500 scale (County Series Second Edition) Cheshire Sheet XXIII. 16. Surveyed 1872, Revised 1897 (Published 1898).

37. Lynch, *Changing Face of Ellesmere Port*, 113; RAF (1947) aerial photographs consulted at Cheshire HER.

38. Building and feature numbers in brackets in the text, e.g. (Building 1), (25) etc. have been allocated to clarify structures on the 1873 map (Figure 5) and subsequent figures.

39. This has been standard practice within Ordnance Survey for large-scale maps and is documented in the Archaeology Division internal rulebook (*c*.1976 – copy in possession of the author) and general background in J.B. Harley, *Ordnance Survey Maps: a Descriptive Manual* (Southampton, 1975), 144–58.

40. OS 1-inch scale First Edition map surveyed *c*.1840 (David and Charles reprint, 1970).

41. Young, *Perambulation of the Hundred of Wirral*, plate facing p. 71.

42. E.W. Cox, 'Stanlaw – a forgotten abbey', *Wirral Notes and Queries*, II (1892), note 124, 68–69.

43. OS 1:2500 scale (County Series Second Edition) Cheshire Sheet XXIII. 16. Surveyed 1872, Revised 1897 (Published

1898); OS 1:2500 scale (County Series Third Edition) Cheshire Sheet XXIII. 16. Surveyed 1872, Revised 1908 (Published 1911).

44. Young, *Perambulation of the Hundred of Wirral*, 73.

45. OS 1:2500 scale (County Series Third Edition) Cheshire Sheet XXIII. 16. Surveyed 1872, Revised 1908 (Published 1911); OS 1:10560 scale (County Series) Cheshire Sheet XXIII. S.E. (Published 1929); OS 1:10560 scale (County Series) Cheshire Sheet XXIII. S.E. (Published 1938). OS 1:10560 scale (County Series) Cheshire Sheet XXIII. S.E. Provisional Edition (Published 1954); OS 1:2500 scale (National Grid Series) SJ 4277 (Published 1959. Surveyed 1958: derived from 1:1250 scale). Maps consulted on English Heritage Geographical Information System database and at CRO.

46. RAF (1947) aerial photographs consulted at Cheshire HER.

47. OS 1:2500 scale (National Grid Series) SJ 4277 (Published 1959. Surveyed 1958: derived from 1:1250 scale). Map consulted at CRO; 1971, 1985, 1999 Cheshire County Council aerial photographs consulted at Cheshire HER.

48. Crowe, 'Numbers 1–4 Stanlow Point'.

49. Williams and MacKinder, 'Draft survey report on Stanlow Abbey'.

50. G. Coppack, *The White Monks: the Cistercians in Britain 1128–1540* (Stroud, 1998), 51–56.

51. C. Platt, *The Abbeys and Priories of Medieval England* (London, 1984), 49 – quoting O. Ashmore, *A Guide to Whalley Abbey* (1968).

2

CURVILINEAR ENCLOSURES IN THE CHESHIRE LANDSCAPE

Anthony Annakin-Smith

This paper considers the form and origins of three large landscape features apparent in a west Cheshire township. Two of the features take the form of curvilinear or 'oval' enclosures whilst a third forms a substantial stock funnel. It will be argued that the features are indicative of a planned medieval landscape which expanded over time. Evidence will be advanced to suggest that, for the larger of the two enclosures, the apogee may have come in the early fourteenth century, but the origin of the managed landscape may be considerably earlier. Parallels with similar enclosures in various parts of England, some of apparent considerable antiquity, will be discussed.

The township of Willaston

The landscape features can be found in the township of Willaston, in the parish of Neston and part of Wirral hundred. There is good evidence for Willaston having been established prior to the Conquest. The Domesday hundred in which Willaston lay – Wilaveston (later Wirral) – was apparently named after the settlement. The 'ton' suffix has Anglo-Saxon origins and Dodgson suggests the place-name means 'Wīglāf's farm' incorporating an OE personal name.[1] The suffix may indicate even earlier origins: Elrington suggests that *tūn* occurs in 'territories previously cleared and kept clear by Romano-British communities'.[2] A Roman road runs through the east of the township (A–B, Figure 1) but no evidence has been

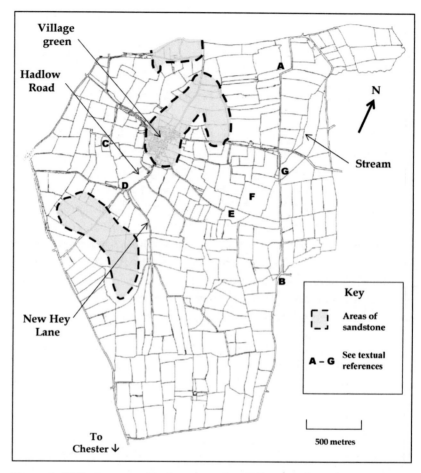

Figure 1. Willaston township based on the Willaston tithe map of 1848, the earliest known complete cartographic depiction of the township.

discovered to date of Romano-British settlement in the immediate area.

The local geology further supports the idea of early settlement as the township contains two large 'islands' of sandstone (Figure 1) covered by relatively thin soils, on slightly elevated ground, within a predominantly clay landscape;[3] such sites were typical of pre-Conquest Wirral settlements.[4]

Despite this evidence, there is no reference to Willaston as a manor in Domesday Book, the first manorial record not occurring until 1230.[5] It has, however, been suggested that the unidentified Wirral Domesday manor of Edelaue, held by Hugh, first earl of Chester, may have been at Willaston.[6] This manor's name has phonetic similarities with Hadlow, an area encompassing the southern sandstone site. However, no trace of a medieval settlement has been found there to date. We cannot be certain, therefore, how many holdings or settlement sites once lay within the township's boundaries. Space does not permit fuller discussion of this issue but there may plausibly have been two areas of settlement within the current township boundaries – Willaston and Edelaue – each of which may have experienced discontinuity of occupation.

The landscape features of Willaston township

The landscape features will be described based on the 1848 tithe map;[7] this shows an almost entirely nucleated settlement centred on a green. Eighteenth-century estate maps show many buildings fronting on to this green, several of which still stand, including the seventeenth-century Old Hall.[8] Some commentators have claimed the green was the hundred court meeting place; others have suggested the meeting place was at Edelaue.[9]

The Willaston enclosure takes the form of a series of linear components in the landscape – lanes and field boundaries. Figure 2 shows these components and suggests how they might once have been joined to create a continuous and substantial curvilinear structure. It takes the form of an offset oval, blunted by the township boundary to the north. This apparent structure includes the present village centre and the northern sandstone 'island'. Excluding the northern border, 70% of the boundary can be traced on the tithe map.

The visible linear features – and thus, this author would argue, the structure as a whole – appear to be primary features in the landscape, as almost all the abutting boundaries terminate against them. The only exceptions are (a) several routeways radiating from the village centre and (b) field boundaries at points where the line of the curvilinear enclosure is lost, suggesting later landscape reorganisation. There is evidence for such reorganisation. For example, between points C and D (Figure 1), the tithe map shows a simple field boundary. But the 1774 estate map shows this was once a lane,[10] and today no boundary exists at all along part of this line. Separately, it seems clear that the southern boundary of field E has been interrupted by the creation of two closes at right angles to the original line. And, at point F, aerial photography shows signs of former ridge and furrow parallel to the line of the suggested missing boundary.[11] It is reasonable to assume, therefore, that other 'missing' sections of the curvilinear enclosure may also have existed as long-gone linear features. Further characteristics of the enclosure include differing field patterns within and outside the boundary, as well as different groups of field names. For example twelve fields with 'Heath' name elements lie immediately outside its eastern side (Figure 2).

Further inspection of the oval reveals several other linear features – lanes, streams and field boundaries – within and more-or-less parallel to the outer boundaries. The Roman road also appears to have been one of these features.[12] Most, if not all, appear to be primary features with very few lines crossing them. The overall impression is of a dynamic landscape, with the oval appearing to represent the outer limit of a series of boundaries pushing towards it from the village centre.

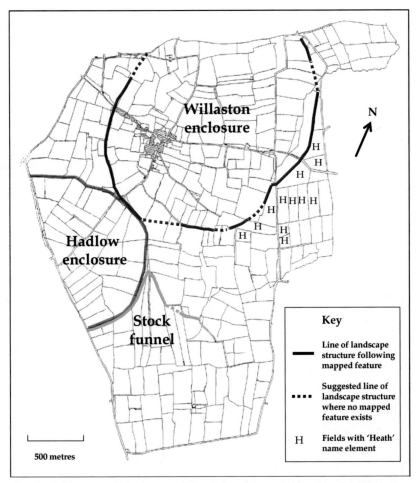

Figure 2. The two enclosures and stock funnel overlaid on to the tithe map. The Willaston enclosure is just over 1.8 km wide by 1.7 m long, oriented north-south, with an area of approximately 265 ha. The smaller Hadlow enclosure is just under 1.5 km along its straight edge, 800 m in radius, and approximately 100 ha in area.

Towards the eastern side of the oval lie two small enclosures (point G, Figure 1), appearing to form the narrowing neck of a funnel, at a point close to which a stream used to rise. This location appears to be 'Stokuuelsiche' ('watercourse at the stock-well'[13]) referred to in an agreement dated 1305.[14] At that time the land to the east of the southern end of the Roman road was heathland, where rights of common grazing pertained. A similar, larger, 'funnel neck' can be made out a few metres further south, the west side forming part of the oval boundary and giving rise to a small diversion in the oval's suggested course. It appears the location of the funnel was moved south as the eastern side of the oval expanded: first the boundary followed the line of the stream, later the boundary shifted eastwards along a broadly parallel line.

The Hadlow enclosure comprises a more-or-less rounded and unbroken semi-circle (Plate 4). Like the Willaston enclosure it encompasses a large area of sandstone, and includes the highest point in the township, potentially of strategic importance. The straight edge runs along the current A540 Chester High Road, a routeway which follows several Wirral township boundaries suggesting it may be of great antiquity. There is no indication today that the arc ever crossed this line into the neighbouring townships of Ness and Burton. Lanes delineate 78% of the curved boundary on the tithe map; a shallow depression along much of the rest of the line today suggests that the lane was once even longer. Again, this curvilinear enclosure appears to be a primary landscape feature. However, unlike the Willaston oval, there is little to suggest that there was a succession of other boundaries either pushing out to or, indeed, beyond it.

The 'Hadlow' area name was first recorded in 1831, appearing to be a variant of an earlier (1714) field name, 'Adlowe', later also mutated to the tithe name 'Adler'.[15] Thirty of the thirty-three substantial fields within this arc include the term 'Adler' (five adjacent fields and two more remote ones also include it).[16] Dodgson gives no firm derivation for the name, but mentions the possible 'Edelaue' link.[17]

At point D, Figure 1, there was once a five-way junction, suggesting that access to this area may have been of some importance.

The stock funnel is a well-formed example of this uncommon lowland landscape feature. Stock funnels provided a link between open grazing land – waste – for livestock and locations where the stock needed to be assembled. Grazing cattle or oxen would be herded from the open land towards the funnel neck for temporary containment or leading elsewhere. This feature indicates that stock-grazing was an important activity in this area at some time. The shape of the Willaston funnel is clear, although a small section of the eastern arm has been broken by later field boundaries. The western arm shares a boundary with the Hadlow curvilinear enclosure. An important feature of many stock funnels was a watering facility for livestock at the mouth. The tithe map shows two water-filled pits at this point, one very large. And the lane, though today called New Hey Lane, was once Newel Lane, judging by several adjacent field names (e.g. 'Newel Lane Adler'). Thus it appears a 'new well' (OE *wælla* – a spring, well or stream) was once to be found here. New Hey Lane gives access to the village centre, via Hadlow Road (Figure 1) along which there is a concentration of ancient farmhouses.

Interpretation
These landscape features can be interpreted in many ways, particularly in the light of Willaston's uncertain early history, and it would be unwise to assume automatically any relationship between the three features, either in function or in their period of origin or use. However, two key points are immediately apparent – their distinct shapes clearly represent

explicit effort to plan the landscape at one or more points in time. It seems implausible that the neat semi-circle of the Hadlow enclosure, the arms of the stock funnel or the more-or-less continuous Willaston oval happened by chance. Further, given the primary nature of the enclosures, this planning must have been in a period before the landscape was broken into closes, a process that was well-advanced locally by the early seventeenth century.[18] A planned approach is evident, separately, in the development of the central settlement of Willaston itself. The site was selected at the highest point of a large sandstone 'island'. The central green, oriented exactly north-south, was marked out at some point, from which no fewer than eight routeways (roads, lanes, and ancient paths) emanate. At least one back lane also radiates from the green. From its earliest days Willaston shows the hand of planning.

Curvilinear enclosures in England
With limited documentary evidence available, it may be helpful to use analogies from elsewhere in order to suggest clues to the interpretation of the Willaston features.

The shapes of the two enclosures are suggestive of many medieval parks across the country. For example, four miles from Willaston lay Shotwick Park, first recorded in the 1320s.[19] It was a similar blunted oval shape to the Willaston enclosure and of similar proportions (approximately 2 kilometres by 2 kilometres) – but there is no documentary evidence that any part of Willaston was ever imparked. Nevertheless, construction of medieval parks shows that landowners were quite capable of conceiving and constructing large enclosures, and also that they recognised that curved boundaries were an economical way of carving up large landscapes, minimising the construction effort and subsequent maintenance required.

Roberts and Wrathmell identified a propensity for 'loop-form' or 'ring-fenced' enclosures in certain areas of England including Cheshire and Lancashire and parts of the east of the country.[20] They conclude that these curvilinear enclosures were agrarian structures and may represent the first 'taking-in of areas of "better land" with the least effort'. They were carved out of woodland, moor or heath leaving areas of common grazing land between them. The dates of origin of these enclosures may vary widely, running from 'pre-medieval to medieval, however this may be defined'. They were 'normally the focus for important farmsteads, halls, and even township or parish foci', but the initial loop forms could lose parts of their definition over time as the worked landscape expanded and was adapted.[21]

Other authors have identified curvilinear enclosures, with apparent varied purposes and origins. In Lancashire and south Cumbria, Atkin identified many examples of 'oval enclosures', usually in pairs – 'double ovals' – interpreted as one arable and one pastoral. However, the term 'oval' can be misleading for they take a variety of shapes, often incorporating irregularities including straight edges.[22] These primary landscape structures could measure almost 2 kilometres in length, and are variously defined by lanes, footpaths, township boundaries and, sometimes, large banks. They typically occurred in upland, forest areas and were often associated with stock funnels. Atkin interpreted them as vaccaries – medieval stock farms. Her view was that the vaccaries' origins may have lain in much earlier double-ovals which had been enclosed from waste. She cites studies of stock management systems with Celtic origins, with possible Roman antecedents. She also noted large oval enclosures in lowland sites, linked to areas of upland grazing. Roberts and Wrathmell cite the Romano-British settlement at Royston Grange, Derbyshire as an apparent example of a

Figure 3. A large curvilinear enclosure at Lathom, Lancashire (cut through by a later canal), a settlement site since the Iron Age.

double-oval arrangement, one pastoral and one arable. In a Cheshire context, and with a rather different interpretation, the same authors cite Sylvester who identified two apparent townfields in Hunsterson township, Wybunbury in a figure of eight formation which the later authors term 'ovals'.[23]

Single ovals may also offer clues to the origins of the Willaston enclosures. Hooke cites Warner who identified rounded single enclosures, up to one kilometre in diameter, in two different Suffolk parishes. These were centred on halls and thus termed 'hall estates' and 'represent manorial demesnes established by late Anglo-Saxon times, their curving ring-fenced boundaries fossilised in present-day field patterns'.[24] Roberts identifies what he believes was a 'pre-1100' oval at Cockfield, County Durham, approximately 550 metres at its longest, described as an 'arable nucleus' with a hall site at its eastern end.[25] Archaeological work in Lancashire, by Philpott and Cowell of Liverpool Museums, has identified many examples of curvilinear enclosures, for example at Lathom (Figure 3), two townships in Knowsley and at Halewood.[26] Some of these sites contain, or are adjacent to, areas of settlement dating back to the Iron Age, as well as being associated with the Romano-British and/or medieval periods.

There are thus numerous precedents for curvilinear enclosures regionally and nationally. However, they cannot be ascribed to any single purpose or period of origin and may have considerable longevity.[27]

Willaston's arable lands

In many of the above examples it appears that at least one of the ovals was used for arable purposes. There are a number of indicators that the large Willaston enclosure was intended or suitable for such use:

• It is close to the centre of Willaston, providing ready access to the crops for those dwelling by the green, the presumed early hub of the settlement;
• It includes an area of sandstone, where lighter soils would have been more easily cleared and worked (supplemented by manuring and marling) than the surrounding heavy clays;
• Field-name evidence suggests this was once the main arable area of land. OE or ME terms typically associated with arable lands – Acre, Land, Butt, Furlong and their variants – occur only within the large oval (the only, notable, exception being the Ness Acre area to the west of the Willaston oval, perhaps indicating a late extension to the arable lands). Town Field references also occur within the oval, near the village centre. Other names within the oval typically have OE or ON

origins, suggesting early naming, whereas those to the south generally do not;
• Field shapes (including aratral curves), particularly to the north east of the village centre and in the Town Field area, are indicative of arable use;
• Traces of ridge and furrow have been identified in many fields within the oval, but in only one outside it, though no attempt has been made to date these.[28]

It is also noticeable that the apparent locations of stock management – the stock funnel to the south, and the eastern 'stock-well' and funnel necks – are either wholly outside the suggested arable area or on the outer side of its expanding boundary.

The great agrarian crisis
It was suggested above that the Willaston enclosure had a series of inner, primary, boundaries. Assuming that this area was an arable enclosure, then the succession of boundaries suggests that it was expanding, presumably to meet the needs of a growing population over time. Logically, the apogee of the arable enclosure is likely to represent the peak of the medieval population which would surely have been in the early fourteenth century.[29] This century saw the devastation of the British population by the Black Death, but an earlier event also had a major impact – an agrarian crisis which led to widespread famine and disease. This arose in a period of substantial deterioration of the weather across Britain and much of Europe, starting in summer 1314 and lasting several years.[30] Unseasonal, torrential rain, cold and windy summers and prolonged bitter winters led to widespread crop failure, consequent famine and associated disease. Murrain also descended.

In Willaston, in 11 Edward II (i.e. 1317–18) the then holders of the manor, Oliver de Burdegalia [Bordeaux] and Matilda his wife, sought permission from Edward earl of Chester (the future King Edward III) for they and their tenants to 'inclose and cultivate the wastes' of the manor.[31] The winter of 1317–18 was the harshest winter of the decade.[32] Thus, a plausible interpretation of the request is that it was a desperate attempt to protect the few crops they were able to grow, and their other limited resources, from game which had a free run of the Forest of Wirral. This enclosure was certainly constructed as, in 1359, the then manor holder successfully appealed against a fine imposed in connection with its existence.[33]

The enclosure's form is unknown. The most effective solution – a bank topped by a pale, with an outer ditch (i.e. like a deer park boundary, but in reverse) – almost certainly required a level of effort unavailable to a severely weakened, maybe reduced, population. In any event earthworks were not necessarily a feature of contemporary local parks – no evidence of earthworks survives along much of Shotwick Park land boundary and 'historical evidence suggests [it] was enclosed by paling'.[34] This method may therefore have been used at Willaston, leaving less enduring traces in the landscape. The limits of this enclosure were unstated but Oliver sought to enclose the 'wastes' indicating that at least part of it was beyond the then arable area. It is possible that the Willaston curvilinear enclosure marks the outer limits of this protected fourteenth-century area.

The weather improved unevenly from 1318, with a return to sustained, more moderate conditions not occurring until 1322.[35] However, the enclosure request at Willaston appears to have succeeded before then for Oliver de Bordeaux sought permission in 1321 to erect a mill in Willaston.[36] This is the first record of such a request locally and suggests that significant quantities of arable crops were now being grown – protected from forest animals and benefiting from some improvement in the weather; these were also good reasons, perhaps, to expand the area under cultivation within the oval to its limits.

Oliver and his wife had manors in other Cheshire forests, and they also sought permission to create enclosures in Blacon, [North] Rode and Ashton near Tarvin.[37] However, this author is yet to find documentary evidence that these were constructed and, whilst elongated curvilinear boundaries can be seen in these townships, additional research is required to see if they could plausibly relate to the fourteenth-century enclosure requests.

The Willaston enclosure's origins

If it is assumed that the Willaston enclosure marks a fourteenth-century apogee to an expanding arable area, where were the earliest lands to be cleared for agricultural use? Any answer is inevitably conjectural but it is possible to pick out several lanes and field boundaries that could form the basis of a roughly curvilinear area encompassing the Willaston sandstone 'island' and from which broadly parallel boundaries could have expanded.

Interestingly, nine of the fields in this central area include the name element 'intake' (Figure 4). This word derives from an ON term, *Inntak*, for an enclosure. The use here is atypical, it more usually being applied to the enclosure of marginal land rather than land at the centre of a settlement.[38] Wirral has many Norse name elements, derived from the settlement of the Hiberno-Norse peoples in the early tenth century; this is the largest and most concentrated use of the term on the peninsula.

The date of construction of a possible 'first enclosure' cannot be ascertained and use of the ON term *Inntak* does not

70

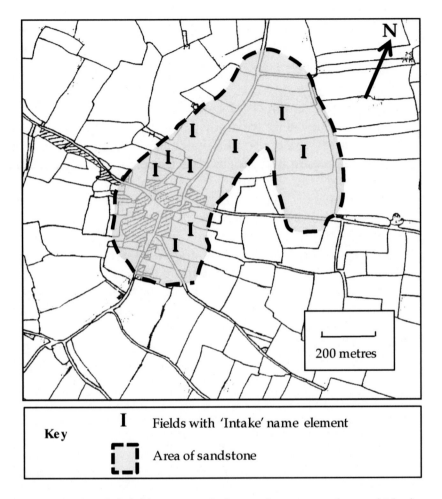

Key

I   Fields with 'Intake' name element

      Area of sandstone

Figure 4. 'Intake' field-names and the sandstone area from which the Willaston enclosure may have expanded.

preclude any such enclosure either post-dating or pre-dating (maybe substantially) the era of Hiberno-Norse settlement. But the presence of a curvilinear enclosure at a place of administrative importance (the hundredal centre), and where there is a hall site, is consistent with observations on pre-Conquest enclosures elsewhere, described earlier.

Origins of the Hadlow enclosure and the stock funnel

If the Willaston enclosure marked arable lands then where was the pasture? At least two main possibilities can be presented: (a) that the Willaston and Hadlow enclosures formed a pair, the latter being the pasture, or (b) that the stock funnel complements the Willaston enclosure, with the Hadlow enclosure being of different origin.

The double-ovals elsewhere were generally conjoined or close together and it could be argued that the Hadlow and Willaston enclosures formed such a pair. But the soil-covered sandstone island of Hadlow is typical of those used for early settlement in Wirral and it seems probable that it became cleared and occupied in pre-Conquest times. It therefore seems less likely to be a pastoral oval, constructed to complement an arable one at Willaston. The carefully demarked semi-circle may, instead, represent the early carving out of arable lands in the manner described by Roberts and Wrathmell, marking a separate manor (or manor-like holding) to Willaston. Philpott suggests that some north-west oval enclosures 'may be small estates of medieval origin'.[39]

If the Hadlow settlement did exist, it shows no signs of longevity or expansion. It had been waste c.1070, following the harrying of the north, and Domesday Book records only a solitary ploughman there. It may have become abandoned in the century after the Conquest, perhaps with the few inhabitants moving to the centre of Willaston. This would have reflected the trend towards settlement nucleation evident in the North West in the post-Conquest period.[40]

This interpretation suggests that the Willaston oval's arable lands and the pasture lands accessed via the stock funnel were complementary in medieval times. The stock funnel may, thus, have been constructed to take advantage of the shape of the Hadlow area. Clearly, for an unknown period, the area south of the funnel was a significant grazing area, for cattle or oxen, but Atkin's upland vaccary model does not fit well with lowland Wirral. Vaccaries were, however, typically sited in forests[41] and Wirral was afforested from the early twelfth century until 1376.[42]

Lowland cattle farms were, however, also an important feature of the medieval Cheshire landscape. For example, the Macclesfield vaccaries were supplied with significant numbers of cattle from some of the earl of Chester's other manors in the 1350s, including Shotwick and Frodsham, and up to 500 cattle were permitted to graze at Poole in 1272.[43] Lords could exploit their grazing land in a variety of ways – demesne grazing, charges to tenants for using the land, and agistment; all or any of these might, perhaps, have applied at Willaston. The presence of the 'stock-well' and apparent funnel necks on the eastern side of the oval further indicate the importance of livestock in medieval Willaston. It appears that at a relatively late date the area south of the New Hey Lane funnel was broken into mostly rectilinear closes which were generally given prosaic names, such as 'Widow's Hey', 'Edwardses', and 'Fox Hey'.

Conclusion

This article has suggested different origins, uses and development histories for the various curvilinear structures visible in Willaston's landscape. It is acknowledged that, with little corroborative documentary evidence, much of the interpretation cannot yet be definitively substantiated. Valuable supporting evidence is likely to be found in analogous landscapes and, as time progresses, it is hoped that further research into curvilinear structures will emerge from other areas.

In a Cheshire context, Willaston is certainly not the only township to contain large curvilinear forms including enclosures. This author has noted many examples in a series of far-from-exhaustive observations across the county. These include near-perfect ovals, lengthy curved boundaries and stock funnels. For example, a well-rounded three-quarter-oval with a 3.7 kilometre near-continuous primary perimeter surrounds the scattered settlement of Mutlow in Gawsworth township.[44] Mutlow may have been a hundredal meeting place (for the later defunct Hamestan hundred)[45] just as Hadlow, lying within another arc, may also have once been such a meeting place. Many apparent links to pastoral activity within the Mutlow oval also merit investigation.

To date, however, no systematic attempt has been made to identify or interpret the range of curvilinear landscape features across Cheshire. As the form, purpose, time of origin and duration of use of these shapes can vary enormously, each one needs individual consideration of its geology, topography, recorded history, archaeology, place-name evidence and relationships to other structures and places, as well as careful new study of cartographic and other archival sources. There is, consequently, the potential for an enormous amount of further research in this wide-ranging and fascinating topic, some of which may help to take us back to the very roots of our communities.[46]

References

1. J. Dodgson, *The Place-Names of Cheshire*, IV (Cambridge, 1972), 232.

2. *VCH Ches*, I, 246.
3. British Geological Survey (2006), 1:50000, Sheet 96, Liverpool.
4. E. Rideout, *The Growth of Wirral* (Liverpool, 1927), 3–6.
5. G. Ormerod, *The History of the County Palatine and City of Chester* [hereafter *History of Cheshire*], II (2nd edn, London, 1882), 544.
6. W. Fergusson Irvine, 'The Domesday survey of the hundred of Wirral', *JCAS*, new ser. V (1893), 81.
7. Willaston tithe map and apportionment (approved 1850): CALS: EDT 430/1–2.
8. Map of Samuel Ryder's Estate, 1774: CALS: DHL 49/3; Map of all the closes belonging to Edmund Lyon, 1745: CALS: DHL 49/1.
9. E.C. Bryan, *Willaston's Heritage* (2nd edn, Willaston, 1997); *VCH Ches*, I, 267.
10. CALS: DHL 49/3.
11. Huntings Surveys Ltd, Run 10, No. 1002, 03/05/1971.
12. K. Jermy, 'The Roman road in Wirral', *JCAS*, new ser. XLVIII (1961), 1–13; K. Jermy, 'The Roman road in Wirral', *JCAS*, new. ser. L (1963), 1–2.
13. Dodgson, *Place-Names of Cheshire*, IV, 234.
14. *Chartulary or Register of Chester Abbey*, ed. J. Tait (Chetham Soc., 2nd ser., 1920–23), I, 97–99.
15. Bryant, *Map* (1831); *Cheshire Sheaf*, 3rd ser. XXX, 6 (1935), 51.
16. Collectively these were sometimes known as 'the Adlers' or 'Adlowes'. A similar field-name element – 'Adlass' – occurs in nearby Leighton township, Neston. Here it is a variant for 'headless' referring to a local stone cross (CALS: DHL 15/2 and DHL 16/5). At Hadlow, it may be relevant that the Wirral Stone, three blocks of sandstone which may once have formed a single elongated sandstone pillar, are

situated adjacent to the enclosure, by the present A540, but its origin is unknown (Cheshire HER 2329).

17. Dodgson, *Place-Names of Cheshire*, IV, 232.
18. G. Chitty, 'Wirral rural fringes survey', *JMAS*, II, 16 (1978), 1–25.
19. Dodgson, *Place-Names of Cheshire*, IV, 210.
20. B. Roberts and S. Wrathmell, *Region and Place* (London, 2002), 158–59. In the North West they depict ring-fenced enclosures as most pronounced in Lancashire; they deem Cheshire a 'challenging sub-province' to interpret, depicting many smaller oval and sub-oval structures.
21. Roberts and Wrathmell, *Region and Place*, 152–53.
22. M. Atkin, 'Some settlement patterns in Lancashire' in D. Hooke, ed., *Medieval Villages, A Review of Current Work* (Oxford, 1985), 179.
23. Roberts and Wrathmell, *Region and Place*, 99.
24. D. Hooke, *The Landscape of Anglo-Saxon England* (London, 1998), 221.
25. B. Roberts, 'Townfield origins: the case of Cockfield, County Durham' in T. Rowley, ed., *The Origins of Open-Field Agriculture* (London, 1981), 145–61.
26. R. Cowell, 'Knowsley rural fringes', *JMAS*, XI (2002), 123–64; R. Cowell and R. Philpott, *Prehistoric, Romano-British and Medieval Settlement in Lowland North West England* (Liverpool, 2000), 205–10; (for Lathom) R. Philpott, personal correspondence, and R. Cowell 'Late prehistoric lowland settlement in North West England' in M. Nevell and N. Redhead, eds, *Mellor: Living on the Edge* (Manchester, 2005), 49–64.
27. Other examples are cited by S. Oosthuizen, 'Medieval field systems and settlement nucleation: common or separate origins?' in N. Higham and M. Ryan, eds, *Landscape*

Archaeology of Anglo-Saxon England (Woodbridge, 2010), 123–26.

28. A. Annakin-Smith, 'The Township of Willaston from Pre-Conquest Times to 1848' (University of Liverpool MA dissertation, 2002). Based on observations made by the author and Hilary Morris.

29. Roberts and Wrathmell, *Region and Place*, 41, citing other sources.

30. G. Mingay, *A Social History of the English Countryside* (London, 1990); W.C. Jordan, *The Great Famine* (Princeton, 1996).

31. HMSO, *Report of the Deputy Keeper of Public Records*, 27 (London, 1866), 121.

32. Jordan, *Great Famine*, 18.

33. HMSO, *Register of Edward the Black Prince*, III (London, 1932), 348; see also P. Booth and A. Carr, eds, *Account of Master John de Burnham the Younger, Chamberlain of Chester* (RSLC, 1991), 182–83.

34. Cheshire HER 2016.

35. Jordan, *Great Famine*, 18.

36. *Cheshire Sheaf*, 3rd ser. XVIII (1921), 89, citing Chester Plea Roll 33, m.11.

37. HMSO, *Report of the Deputy Keeper*, 121. Note that Ormerod apparently incorrectly post-dates the requests in respect of Rode and Ashton by two years.

38. J. Dodgson, *The Place-Names of Cheshire*, V, S.1:ii (Cambridge, 1981), 250; R. Kain and C. Prince, *The Tithe Surveys of England and Wales* (Cambridge, 1985), 163.

39. Cowell and Philpott, *Prehistoric, Romano-British and Medieval Settlement*, 209.

40. R. Britnell, *Britain and Ireland 1050–1530* (Oxford, 2004), 23–27; N. Higham, *A Frontier Landscape, The North West in the Middle Ages* (Macclesfield, 2004), 126–29.

41. See, for example, P. Booth, ed., *Accounts of the Manor and Hundred of Macclesfield, Cheshire, Michaelmas 1361 to Michaelmas 1362* (RSLC, 2003), xxxiii.
42. *VCH Ches*, II, 184–85.
43. Booth, *Accounts*, xxvi; H. Hewitt, *Mediaeval Cheshire* (Manchester, 1929), 49.
44. Clearly visible on the OS 6-inch map, sheet 43 (1871).
45. A. Phillips and C. Phillips, *A New Historical Atlas of Cheshire* (Chester, 2002), 26.
46. The author would like to thank the following for their assistance in the preparation of this article: Graeme White, Rob Philpott, Ron Cowell, Hilary Morris. Also thanks to Jen Lewis who first encouraged my investigations into oval enclosures.

3

SETTLEMENTS AND THEIR SHAPES IN NORTH-EAST WALES

Mike Headon

Areas of dispersed settlement were not well served by settlement studies for most of the previous century; while complicated typologies were constructed for the forms of nucleated villages,[1] dispersed settlements were lumped together as a homogeneous mass, the default option. However, since the 1980s more attention has been paid to morphological variations in dispersed settlements and their complicated relationships with nucleated settlements.[2] In addition, the study of landscape history in Wales has been somewhat neglected and consequently is less developed than in England. This paper is a small contribution to redressing the balance.

For the purposes of this paper, the chosen study area is north-east Wales, the pre-1974 counties of Denbighshire and Flintshire.[3] Geographically, this area falls into ten fairly well-defined areas (Figure 1): (1) the coastal strip; (2) the Conway valley; (3) north-west Denbighshire; (4) Mynydd Hiraethog (the Denbigh Moors); (5) the Vale of Clwyd; (6) the Clwydian range; (7) the Berwyn range and Ceiriog valley; (8) the Tanat valley; (9) the Flintshire and Denbighshire coalfield; (10) the Vale of Dee. Figure 2 shows the sites mentioned in the text.

Wales was divided into cantrefi; each cantref was subdivided into commotes. Before the Norman conquest of North Wales in 1282–84, the cantrefi of Rhos and Rhufoniog (roughly, north and west Denbighshire and south and east Denbighshire respectively), the cantref of Tegeingl (north

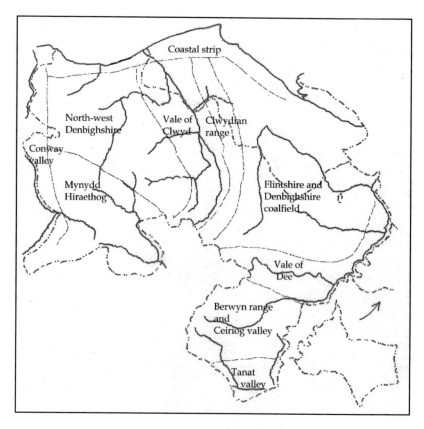

Figure 1. The study area: the pre-1974 counties of Denbighshire and Flintshire.

Flintshire), and the lordship of Dyffryn Clwyd formed part of the principality of Gwynedd, while the south-eastern part of the study area formed the lands known as Powys Fadog, whose rulers were subject to the rulers of Gwynedd. Following Edward I's conquest, the county of Flintshire was created in 1284 out of the commote of Tegeingl, the lordships of Mold and Hope, and the detached area known as Maelor Saesneg or English Maelor. It was not until the Act of Union in 1536 that

Figure 2. Places mentioned in the text.

the county of Denbighshire was created out of the remaining areas: the lordship of Denbigh (the cantrefi of Rhos and Rhufoniog, and the commote of Dinmael from the cantref of Penllyn in the south), the lordship of Dyffryn Clwyd or Rhuthun, and the lordship of Bromfield and Yale and the lordship of Chirk, that together had developed from Powys Fadog.

81

The term 'settlement' may refer to a city, a town, a village, a hamlet, or a farmstead, as well as to specialised establishments such as forts. The differences between them are usually held to be significant in settlement studies. Richard Jones, for example, is exercised to distinguish between hamlets and villages. He quotes the formula 'a village comprises 6 to 60 households, 30 to 300 people';[4] he raises the question 'how close [do] farmsteads need to stand together before they are considered to make up part of a hamlet rather than independent units in their own right?'[5] Indeed, the very title of the key study *Village, Hamlet and Field*[6] cries out for the writer's pen to inscribe '... *and Farmstead*' rather than '... *and Field*'.

All this raises two issues. Firstly, it betrays a mode of thought that is still focusing on nucleated settlements rather than dispersed. Jones goes on to solve his own problem by declaring that a hamlet 'will always have exhibited some signs of social, economic or religious dependence on another place'[7] – it may have had a chapel of ease rather than a parish church; it may have had two or more farmsteads but a narrower range of services. Jones, however, is dealing with settlement desertion, where the differences are of greater importance.

Secondly, is it important when studying settlement formation to distinguish between the different types of settlement, except for the purposes of classification? One aspect that we are unable to take into account, because of the transitory nature of the evidence, is what terms the inhabitants themselves used to describe the place where they lived; and even if we could, we would then face the difficulty of recovering information about how the same term might be assigned a different value at different times. Glanville Jones suggested, for example, that 'it is likely ... that the hamlet of the Survey of Denbigh[8] should be equated with the vill of the law-books and that in some cases the vill of the Survey ... should be equated with the *maenol'*.[9] The histories of the developments in meaning of the OE place-name element *tūn*,[10] and the Welsh *pentre*,[11] both very common in the study area, are long and complicated. In the twenty-first century, houses in a 'village' will often fetch higher prices than those in a town; a small town may have grown considerably in size and yet have metamorphosed into a 'village' on estate agents' websites. Caerleon in south Wales had its own Urban District Council until 1974, and still has a Town Hall; the main settlement is on the west bank of the River Usk, while 'The Village' was a specific place-name (still shown on OS maps), in common use in the mid-twentieth century, referring to the area east of the river. The main settlement is now universally called 'the village'.[12]

How do we know that a settlement did not have a completely different form at some time in the past? This question is unanswerable in absolute terms. We have documentary evidence from the thirteenth century onwards concerning the development of some planned settlements – Edwardian boroughs, the emparkment of gentry-houses, industrial housing, Victorian seaside resorts – as well as documentary evidence in the form of maps and written local histories that tells us something about the development of unplanned settlements in the last two hundred years or so. Earlier than this, we depend on a mixture of theorising and the minimal hard evidence prized by archaeology. It is now generally accepted that nucleated settlements in England are not a naturally occurring phenomenon, but that settlement in the early middle ages was practically universally dispersed, and that there was a shift to nucleation in England, for reasons that are not fully understood, at some time between the ninth and twelfth centuries.[13] Could it be that a subsequent reverse process took place in Wales (or England), where servile groups living together as bond settlements may have disappeared with the disappearance of bond tenure, leaving only an administrative name attached to a farmstead or a group of farmsteads as evidence, as suggested by Glanville Jones?[14]

Clearly, a list of settlement-names to be examined must allow for a range of possibilities. The method adopted for the study was to assemble a corpus of place-names consisting of (1) all names in the study area on the OS 1:25000 map of Wales; (2) all ancient parish and chapelry names; (3) township names in Flintshire (township names are less significant in Denbighshire); (4) Domesday manors – the Domesday survey covered most of Flintshire and a small part of Denbighshire;[15] (5) vills in the Survey of the Honour of Denbigh (1334)[16] – this covers much of Denbighshire, and its shortcomings are similar to those faced when using Domesday Book as a source; (6) places shown on Speed's maps of Denbighshire and Flintshire of 1612, which drew on Saxton's maps of 1579; (7) all places in the comprehensive survey of historic settlements carried out by the Clwyd-Powys Archaeological Trust in 1992–95. The settlement represented by each name in the list was then located and examined on the first-edition OS 6-inch map of the second half of the nineteenth century.

But in an area where most settlement is dispersed, how do we ascertain where the boundary lies between one settlement and another? The limits of a dispersed settlement do not necessarily correspond with formal administrative boundaries. Richard Jones has criticised 'the long-standing obsession historians, archaeologists and geographers have had with physical form as the principal means of categorising rural settlement'.[17] A settlement might be defined by possession of its own sense of identity encapsulated in having its own name; in some sparsely populated parts of the study area, this is illustrated by two or three farmsteads sharing the same name, and this aspect has been regarded as a specific determiner and incorporated into the results below. Ideally, we would carry out detailed research to ascertain how interactions between neighbours take place, and base our boundaries on that. Even so, people interact in different ways, and assign different boundaries to different modes of behaviour. This is not practicable, and the only available evidence is in the form of maps, place-names, and local taxes such as tithes or rates. There are difficulties in using all these sources. With regard to tithes or rates, the local parish is an obvious tax boundary, but, particularly in Denbighshire, a large number of parishes do not have their main village associated with the church. There may be a hamlet attached to the church, but this is often less significant than the other hamlets found in the parish at road junctions and stream- and river-crossings. These hamlets themselves have unclear boundaries; as a rule of thumb, in this study a building more than 400 metres away from the nucleus of a hamlet has not been considered to be part of it.

An additional complication in areas such as the study area, especially to the west and south of Denbighshire, is the question of transhumance, and the relationship between *hendre* and *hafod*; the original meaning of these terms being that a *hendre* was the 'winter dwelling located in the valley to which the family and its stock returned after transhumance during the summer months in the *hafod* on the mountain'.[18] Is the *hafod*, or a group of *hafodydd*, therefore to be regarded as a separate settlement in its own right? There are forty-six occurrences of the element *hendre* in place-names on OS 1:25000 maps of the study area, 123 of the element *hafod*. The deserted settlement of Hafod-y-nant-criafolen D/SH9857[19] was a group of seven buildings, six spread across an area 120 metres long and each with its associated enclosures, focused on a stream confluence.[20] As transhumance decayed, other *hafodydd* were converted into permanent steadings, as demonstrated by the place-name evidence.[21]

The nucleus of a hamlet may be a place of worship such as a church or Nonconformist chapel; it may be a gentry-house; it may be a stream- or river-crossing; it may be a road junction; it may be present but harder to pinpoint, as in streamside settlements or a hamlet grouped around an industrial complex. The nucleus, whatever its physical form, will be a meeting-point, and so will act as a focus for the buildings of social interaction (BSIs) that may have existed since medieval times (the inn, the mill, the smithy) or that have come into existence in modern times (the post office, the vicarage or rectory, the dissenters' chapel, the school, the turnpike). In an area of dispersed settlement, the map may show other buildings, but often it is difficult to discern if these are separate dwellings, or outhouses associated with BSIs. Nevertheless, it is reasonable to assume that the more of these additional buildings there are, the more the settlement is tending towards nucleation. Other non-built structures of the agricultural economy, such as greens, droveways[22] and stock funnels, may also be significant but are not always identifiable in relict form.

When the list of places in the corpus was compared with the shape of the settlement as shown on the first edition OS 6-inch map, nine classes of determiner were identified, as shown in Table 1. The determiners refer mainly to the relationship of the buildings of the settlement with each other, with some reference to roads and streams. Only physical evidence is considered at this stage. Some attempt will be made in the remainder of this paper to indicate how the taxonomy shown in Table 1 was developed (this is displayed on the following pages 87–89).

1   Single farmstead or house
     1.1   without administrative status
     1.2   with administrative status

2   Gentry-house with or without administrative status

2a   Gentry-house with BSIs (buildings of social interaction)

3   Group of farmsteads
     3.1   Uchaf-canol-isaf type
     3.2   Mawr-bach type

4   Church-settlements
     4.1   Lone church
     4.2   Church with BSIs only
     4.3   Church with BSIs and not more than five others
     4.4   Church with BSIs and not more than ten others

5   Church-settlements with gentry-house close by
     5.1   Lone church with gentry-house close by
     5.2   Church with BSIs only with gentry-house close by
     5.3   Church with BSIs and not more than five others with
           gentry-house close by
     5.4   Church with BSIs and not more than ten others with
           gentry-house close by

6   Church-settlements with gentry-house further off
     6.1   Lone church with gentry-house further off
     6.2   Church with BSIs only with gentry-house further off
     6.3   Church with BSIs and not more than five others with
           gentry-house further off
     6.4   Church with BSIs and not more than ten others with
           gentry-house further off

6a   Multiple hamlets (proto-multi-focal)

7   Stream- or river-crossing
     7.1   single route with church-settlement
     7.2   single route without church
     7.3   focus of routes with church-settlement
     7.4   focus of routes without church

8 Road junctions (focus of routes)
  8.1 buildings cluster at junction, with church-settlement
  8.2 buildings cluster at junction without church
  8.3 buildings extend along more than one road, with
    church-settlement
  8.4 buildings extend along more than one road, without
    church

8a Radial settlement

9 Street-village
  9.1 continuous single row
  9.2 interrupted single row

10 Multiple-row

11 Streamside settlement (Tanat valley type)

12 Other dispersed settlement
  12.1 organic dispersed settlement
    12.1.1 density 1
    12.1.2 density 2
    ...
    12.1.n density n

  12.2 dispersed industrial settlements
    12.2.1 narrowly dispersed?
    12.2.2 widely dispersed?

  12.3 common-edge settlements
    12.3.1 original
    12.3.2 replacing earlier settlement

13 Organic agglomeration (nucleated)
  13.1 non-industrial
  13.2 industrial

14 Planned
  14.1 medieval
    14.1.1 grid (rigid or less rigid)

14.2 nineteenth-century seaside development
14.2.1   formal (grid)
14.2.2   informal
14.3 industrial
14.3.1   formal (grid)
14.3.2   informal

Table 1. Taxonomy of settlement types in north-east Wales.

1. *Single farmsteads and houses*

These may be isolated farmsteads, owing their place in the corpus to the map-maker's desire to populate the blank areas on the map, such as Maes-mynan D/SJ1172 – examples are more numerous in Denbighshire, where there is more remote country, than in Flintshire; a simple farmstead carrying an administrative name (Esgair-ebrill D/SH8168 is a vill named in the Survey of the Honour of Denbigh; Bodeugan F/SJ0575 and Cyrchynan F/SJ0475 are Domesday manors); or a larger gentry-house, with substantial areas of grounds attached, frequently emparked, and with a name usually associated with an administrative area (Erddig D/SJ3248).

2. *Grouped farmsteads and houses*

Where a modern map-name corresponds to a medieval name, was it a settlement, or simply an administrative unit? It is common in the study area to find two, three or more farmsteads with the same name, distinguished by *mawr* (big, great) and *bach* (little) – usually within 1500 metres of each other – or, more frequently, by *uchaf* (upper, 'farther'), *canol* (middle), *isaf* (lower, 'nearer'). The base name is frequently associated with an administrative area such as a vill or manor. Bodrochwyn D/SH9373 is an example of the first type, Llwydcoed D/SH8376 and Brynffanigl D/SH9175 of the second.

3. Hamlets, parishes and churches

The parish church is not frequently the focus of a large settlement in the study area. A church may stand completely alone,[23] as at Llanarmon Mynydd Mawr D/SJ1328. There may be a church with BSIs only, as at Llanfynydd F/SJ2756 (Figure 3); with BSIs and not more than five other buildings, as at Efenechtyd D/SJ1155 and Llanfair Dyffryn Clwyd D/SJ1355; or with BSIs and not more than ten other buildings, as at Treuddyn F/SJ2558. If there are more than ten other buildings, we are probably dealing with the germ of a nucleated village.

There may be a gentry-house in close proximity to (within 400 metres of) the church (Llan-rhudd D/SJ1456, Llanrhaeadr-yng-Nghinmeirch D/SJ0863), or further away. In fact, the church may not be there at all: Allington D/SJ3857 is an example of a gentry-house with BSIs but no church. If a number of hamlets, including the church-settlement, are in close proximity, as at Llanelidan D/SJ1050, then we have the germ of a multi-focal settlement.

4. Geographical determiners

Churches are frequently sited near river-crossings and stream-crossings, road junctions, or holy wells, but these can also act as a focus without a church. A river-crossing may service a single route, as at Llanddulas D/SH-9078, but more often routes focus on the crossing from different directions, as at Bont-newydd D/SJ0170 (Figures 4 and 5). Mochdre D/SH8278 is an example of a stream-crossing. Road junctions may be a true crossroads or a three-, four-, five- or six-way junction. Dwellings cluster around the junction itself at Cerrigydrudion D/SH9548 and Rhuallt F/SJ0775, or may extend along some of the routes leading to the junction, as at Trelawnyd F/SJ0979 and Gwytherin D/SH8761. Nonconformist chapels are often sited at

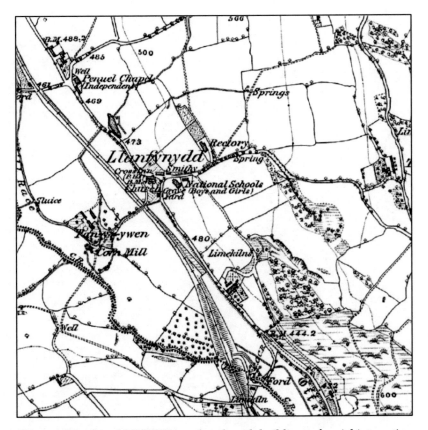

Figure 3. Llanfynydd F/SJ2756: a church with buildings of social interaction only.

road junctions; an example giving its name to a settlement is Nebo D/SH8356 (at 300 metres above sea level, the reference is also to the view of the promised land vouchsafed to Moses from Mount Nebo). If a settlement spreads out along all the arms of a multi-way junction, we can define a radial settlement – rare in the study area, but found at Hope F/SJ3058. The significance of holy wells has not yet been investigated, though

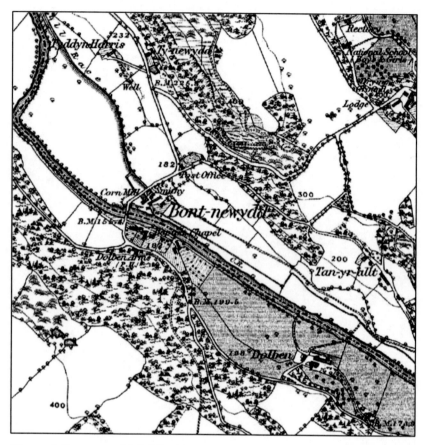

Figure 4. Bont-newydd D/SJ0170: a stream-crossing on the Elwy with routes converging from different directions.

a number occur in the study area, for example Holywell F/SJ1876 and Llandegla D/SJ1952.

5. Street-villages

Settlements located along a single street or lane, with some space between the buildings, giving an interrupted row, are

Figure 5. Bont-newydd (Figure 4) in about 1885, looking south across the bridge over the Elwy, where routes from Cefn Meiriadog, St Asaph/Llanelwy, Henllan and Llanefydd converge.

fairly common in the study area, and are found at Capel Garmon D/SH8155 and Meliden F/SJ0681. A continuous row with no gaps is rarer, though Trefnant D/SJ0570 and Gresford D/SJ3454 are possible examples. A few villages in Flintshire, such as Northop F/SJ2468 and Caergwrle F/SJ3057, correspond more closely to Roberts's multiple-row type.[24]

6. Streamside settlements

The Tanat valley is remote from the rest of the study area, and in its upper reaches has long valleys trending in one direction only, with very high ground inhibiting communication between them. Here settlements consist of fewer than half a dozen buildings on one bank of a stream, with few buildings of social interaction. The settlement-name does not usually have significant administrative status; there is usually a stream-crossing and a junction of very minor local routes. Examples are Rhiwlas D/SJ1932 (the Ogau) and Rhydycroesau D/SJ2430 (the Cynllaith). This type also occurs in the upper valleys of the Dee system, as at Pont-fadog D/SJ2338 (the Ceiriog). This type is not found in Flintshire, due to the absence of such streams.

7. Other dispersed settlements

It might seem that dispersed settlements could be distinguished by density of settlement, but this would be arbitrary and would not reflect variations within the boundaries, and so the general category of *organic dispersed settlement* is defined, as in the parishes of Llanferres D/SJ1860 and Llanychan D/SJ1161. Another type common in the study area is the *narrowly dispersed industrial settlement*. Here, a large number of buildings are constructed, usually during the nineteenth century, in close proximity to each other but not adjacent, with new tracks created to link them. Plate 5 illustrates a settlement of this type at Trefor Uchaf D/SJ2442. Though they are often popularly

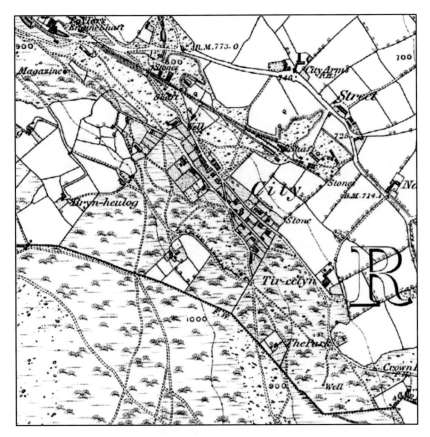

Figure 6. New Brighton (formerly City Lands) D/SJ2750: a narrowly dispersed industrial settlement, in an area of intensive lead and zinc mining.

regarded as squatter settlements, it has been suggested by Robert Silvester (Clwyd-Powys Archaeological Trust)[25] that it is more likely that they represent an attempt by the landholders to exploit surface areas close to but inappropriate for quarrying or the sinking of shafts. Their names are often ironic: New Brighton D/SJ2750 (Figure 6; originally City Lands, bequeathed to the City Charity of Chester), Southsea D/SJ3051; or derived

95

Figure 7. St Asaph/Llanelwy F/SJ0474: an organic native borough.

from chapels: Carmel F/SJ1676. *Widely dispersed industrial settlements* might be distinguished using similar criteria, but this is a matter for further investigation. Common-edge settlements are not necessarily industrial, but those in the study area are generally associated with quarrying or mining: either newly created, as at Marian Cwm F/SJ0777, or replacing an older settlement form as at Llysfaen D/SH8877.

8.   Organic agglomerations
These are nucleated settlements based on agglomeration. The primitive structure cannot usually be recovered; they are less common in the study area than in areas of high nucleation. They can be divided into non-industrial – more ancient, as at Henllan D/SJ0268 – and industrial types, the latter more common in the eastern part of the study area, as at the adjacent but distinct settlements of Rhosymedre and Cefn-mawr, both D/SJ2842.

9.   Planned settlements
The term 'planned' is used with some circumspection these days, as it is now accepted that all settlement development must be the result of planning of some sort, and not necessarily imposed from above: Dyer speaks of 'impetus towards the creation of settlements from below',[26] and as early as 1914 Vinogradoff and Morgan of 'manifestations of the "village community" principle' in discussing the tenurial history of Mochdre D/SH8278.[27] However, alternative terms such as 'regular' carry their own ambiguities.

There are three types of known deliberately planned settlement within the study area:

(a) *Medieval*. The alien borough of Flint F/SJ2472 is the classic example of an Edwardian grid pattern, and the same is found at Holt D/SJ4154, while the native towns of Llanrwst D/SH8062 and St Asaph/Llanelwy F/SJ0474 (Figure 7) exhibit a rather more organic appearance.

(b) *Nineteenth-century seaside developments*. Colwyn Bay D/SH-8579 and Rhyl F/SJ-0081 exhibit a grid pattern, while other developments followed a more informal approach.

(c) *Planned industrial settlements*. These are similar, in that they follow either a grid pattern as at Leeswood F/SJ2759 and

Pentre-rhwygwr (Halton) D/SJ3040, or a more flexible approach.

In summary, a set of significant sources for the construction of a list of place-names has been identified, and a corpus of place-names constructed. The shape of each settlement or place as it was in the later nineteenth century has then been inspected, paying particular attention to the relationship between the buildings in the settlement and the landscape immediately surrounding it. Patterns have been identified and the taxonomy shown in Table 1 constructed. The necessary next step in this research will be to examine a representative sample from each class of the taxonomy to determine whether there is any commonality of tenurial history, geographical or geological determiners, exploitation of the land and its resources, or other natural or social phenomena that can show us what factors might have influenced the development of a settlement's shape in a particular direction.

References
1. Cf. B.K. Roberts, *The Making of the English Village* (Harlow, 1987).
2. Cf. R. Jones and M. Page, *Medieval Villages in an English Landscape: Beginnings and Ends* (Bollington, 2006); C. Lewis, P. Mitchell-Fox and C. Dyer, *Village, Hamlet and Field: Changing Medieval Settlements in Central England* (Manchester, 1997; rev. edn, Bollington, 2001); B.K. Roberts and S. Wrathmell, *An Atlas of Rural Settlement in England* (2nd edn, London, 2003).
3. These counties have different boundaries from the present (2011) unitary authorities of Denbighshire and Flintshire.
4. Lewis *et al.*, *Village, Hamlet and Field*, 5.

5. R. Jones, 'Contrasting patterns of village and hamlet desertion in England' in C. Dyer and R. Jones, eds, *Deserted Villages Revisited* (Hatfield, 2010), 8–27; at 11.
6. Lewis *et al.*, *Village, Hamlet and Field*.
7. Jones, 'Contrasting patterns', 14.
8. *Survey of the Honour of Denbigh 1334*, ed. P. Vinogradoff and F. Morgan (London, 1914).
9. G.R.J. Jones, 'The pattern of medieval settlement in the commote of Rhos Is Dulas and its antecedents' in W. Pinkwart, ed., *Genetische Ansätze in der Kulturlandschaftsforschung: Festschrift für Helmut Jäger* (Würzburger Geographische Arbeiten Heft 60, Würzburg, 1983), 41–50; at 43.
10. A.H. Smith, *English Place-Name Elements, part II* (Cambridge, 1987), 188–98.
11. H.W. Owen, *The Place-Names of East Flintshire* (Cardiff, 1994), 406.
12. For example, 'situated in a central village location' (High Street), 'located in the charming old village of Caerleon' (Isca Road), 'just outside Caerleon village' (College Crescent) – all streets are on the west bank. Rightmove estate agents' website <<http://www.rightmove.co.uk/property-for-sale/Caerleon.html>> accessed 08/11/11.
13. Jones and Page, *Medieval Villages*, 6–8.
14. G.R.J. Jones, 'The distribution of bond settlement in north-west Wales', *Welsh Historical Review*, II: 1 (1964), 19–36.
15. *Domesday Book: Cheshire*, ed. P. Morgan (Chichester, 1978).
16. *Survey of the Honour of Denbigh*.
17. Jones, 'Contrasting patterns', 12.
18. Owen, *Place-Names*, 381–82.
19. The four-figure (one kilometre square) OS grid reference is preceded by D/ for Denbighshire or F/ for Flintshire.

20. R. Silvester, 'Deserted rural settlements in central and north-east Wales' in K. Roberts, ed., *Lost Farmsteads: Deserted Rural Settlements in Wales*, CBA Research Report 148: York, 2006), 13–39; at 35.

21. M. Griffiths, 'The emergence of the modern settlement pattern, 1450–1700' in D.H. Owen, ed., *Settlement and Society in Wales* (Cardiff, 1989), 225–48; at 232.

22. As noted (together with churches) by C. Dyer, 'Medieval settlement in Wales: a summing up' in N. Edwards, ed., *Landscape and Settlement in Medieval Wales* (Oxford, 1997), 165–68; at 165.

23. Strictly speaking, not a settlement, but included for completeness.

24. Roberts, *Making of the English Village*, 26–27 (Figure 2.3).

25. R. Silvester, *Deserted Medieval and Later Rural Settlements in Powys and Clwyd: the Final Report* (Welshpool, 2001).

26. Dyer, 'Medieval settlement in Wales', 167.

27. *Survey of the Honour of Denbigh.*

4

THE ENCLOSURE OF WEST CHESHIRE: KEEPING AHEAD OF 'CHAMPION ENGLAND'

Graeme J. White

During his travels through England and Wales in Henry VIII's reign the king's librarian, John Leland, often noted the character of the countryside through which he was passing. A frequent observation related to whether the landscape was 'champion' or 'enclosed': Oswestry, for example, was described as 'on a plain in a valley 12 long miles by champain having almost no wood', while the land between Preston and Garstang was 'the most part ... enclosures for pasturages'.[1] This distinction was also familiar to William Harrison, for much of Elizabeth I's reign rector of Radwinter and vicar of Wimbish in north-west Essex, so on the frontier between two of the three regions into which English Heritage's *Atlas of Rural Settlement* divides England: to his west was the 'Central Province' characterised by nucleated villages and extensive open arable fields largely worked in common – 'champion country' – to his east the 'South-Eastern Province' with its dispersed hamlets and small pockets of arable strips interspersed with patches of woodland, pasture and meadow, some held in common, some enclosed for exclusive use.[2] 'Our soil being divided into champaign ground and woodland', he wrote, 'the houses of the first lie uniformly builded in every town together with streets and lanes, whereas in the woodland countries (except here and there in great market towns) they stand scattered abroad, each one dwelling in the midst of his own occupying'.[3]

Harrison is often quoted in discussions of the sixteenth-century rural landscape. Less frequently observed is that this sentence is set within a passage lamenting the effects of the engrossing of holdings into the hands of a wealthy few, in terms which echoed the phraseology of several critics of depopulating enclosure, among them the Warwickshire chantry priest John Rous in the late fifteenth century and Thomas More in *Utopia* in 1516. According to Harrison, this 'grievous ... inconvenience, growing ... by encroaching and joining of house to house and laying land to land' applied in different settlement contexts, since 'whether they be woodland or champaign ... the ground of the parish is gotten up into a few men's hands, yea sometimes into the tenure of one, two or three, whereby the rest are compelled either to be hired servants unto the other, or else to beg their bread in misery'.[4] In other words, the consolidation of holdings, seen as a prelude to enclosure and the social evils which followed, applied both in areas where farming had customarily been carried out in great open fields and in areas where it had not.

William Harrison's characterisation of two principal types of landscape, reinforced by the categorisation of England as three great provinces in the *Atlas of Rural Settlement*, shapes much of what is written on these subjects in the early twenty-first century. For Cheshire, however, all this is of limited value, and those who study the county today need to beware of trying to force it into pre-existing models, whether they date from the reign of the first Queen Elizabeth or the second. The *Atlas* duly places the county within its remaining province, the 'Northern and Western', embracing the North West, Welsh marches and most of the West Country, a landscape like the 'South-Eastern' largely characterised by dispersed settlement, small open fields and areas of woodland, pasture and meadow. In subdividing these great provinces into smaller units, it awards Cheshire (plus a tongue extending into Derbyshire and Staffordshire) its own 'Cheshire Plain Sub-Province', only then to describe this as something of an awkward fit: 'a challenging sub-province' where 'the settlement is by no means uniform' and small open fields occur in a context of both villages and hamlets.[5] As for John Leland, he declined to report on whether he found the Cheshire countryside through which he passed to be 'champion' or 'enclosed', possibly because he encountered an irregular pattern of open fields and closes which did not strike him as fitting either description very well. What he did say, as he travelled north from Ridley to Bunbury past Spurstow along what is now the A49, is that there were 'in the fields marvellous good corn and pastures': in other words, variety.[6] In reality, Cheshire's medieval and early-modern landscape was too complex to be defined simply as nucleated or dispersed, open or enclosed: one's inclination to describe it as either 'champaign ground or woodland' would depend on where one was looking.

There was of course nothing inherently superior about the 'champion country' of the 'Central Province', despite its popular association with 'the heart of village England' and a tendency in some literature to imply that regions which did not adopt this form of land management were somehow less favoured and behind the times.[7] The connotations of the word 'champion' do nothing to dispel these illusions. The term derives from the Latin *campus*, used in medieval documents to mean an 'open field' but also the root of the Middle English word which meant 'master of the fighting field'. In reality, life within 'champion country' was for many a desperate struggle, since communities where up to 90% of the available land was given over to open arable fields stretching to the township boundaries, at the expense of essential resources of common pasture, meadow and woodland – as was the case in the midland clay vales of Northamptonshire and south-eastern Warwickshire by the end of the thirteenth century – had a severely unbalanced local economy. There is much to suggest that in the more varied farming regimes of the western and eastern shires there was greater opportunity for enterprise, and better living standards for the majority of those directly reliant on the land, than was the case in 'Champion England'. That enterprise is nowhere better demonstrated than in the enclosure of the open fields.

By the eighteenth and early nineteenth centuries, as all students of the Agricultural Revolution are well aware, criticism of communal open field farming in strips was widespread. Parliamentary Enclosure Acts routinely opened with a statement to the effect that 'by reason of the different interests [of] the several land owners and occupiers, or persons having right of common' the fields 'cannot be improved, cultivated or enjoyed ... as they might be and are capable of'.[8] Such sentiments were nothing new but, as Christopher Dyer has demonstrated, it was mainly outside rather than within the 'champion' zone that there was an early drive towards enclosure of open strips and common pasture in pursuit of individual advantage.[9] West Cheshire shared in this enterprise, and in that sense kept itself ahead of 'Champion England', where communal regulations inevitably acted as a brake upon individualism and where, in many midland counties, around half the land surface eventually had to be subjected to parliamentary enclosure in order to be rid of the open fields and their accompanying commons. But parliamentary enclosure was an admission of failure, an acknowledgement that binding agreements to a reallocation of previously-shared land could only be achieved through expensive resort to legislation and the engagement of external commissioners and a surveyor. With certain exceptions, this is what the landowners of Cheshire managed to avoid.

The widespread occurrence within Cheshire of some form of farming in strips, in the middle ages or later, has been known for over half a century and tell-tale references to open strips as 'selions', 'butts', 'loons', 'quillets' or (in some contexts) 'lands', to blocks of strips as 'flatts' or 'furlongs', and to a community's principal or only open field as the 'town field' have continued to be found over much of the county, not least by members of the Chester Society for Landscape History whose first quarter-century is being celebrated here.[10] The *New Historical Atlas of Cheshire* in 2002 reckoned that there was evidence of former open fields, however small, in some 180 townships, almost two-thirds of them in west Cheshire, defined for present purposes by a line running due south from the mouth of the River Weaver so embracing Wirral, the Dee-Gowy lowlands and the mid-Cheshire ridge.[11] There can no longer be any doubt that throughout this area open field farming was a familiar feature of the medieval landscape, even if not as dominant as in 'Champion England': townships which never had any open field farming whatsoever were exceptional.

We know little in detail about how these open fields were worked, although we must presume that, as in the 'champion' zone, their management was intimately bound up with that of communally-accessed meadow and pasture. In 1297, three-course rotations were operating in Tarvin and Wybunbury, although covering a multiplicity of small open fields in each township, not two, three or four great ones as in much of the midlands.[12] A grant of June 1393 to William, son of Hugh Barnston, of various butts in the fields of Churton suggests that they had originally been distributed according to a repetitive sequence, probably reflecting the order in which house-plots were held, since most of the butts were described as either lying between the land of William de Boston on one side and the land of John Sandall on the other, or had at least one of them as neighbour. Entitlements to open arable strips certainly carried common grazing rights with them: a rental relating to Tilston in 1559 explains that three 'loondes' (or strips) in the town fields made an acre, and that for every loonde held it was customary to let one beast into the town fields once the corn had been harvested. In the seventeenth and well into the eighteenth century, the manorial court of Alvanley was busily regulating pasture-rights and enforcing communal obligations to maintain the hedges, gutters and roadways which served the open fields: in October 1665, for example, six men were fined ten shillings each for carting grass away from the common pastures, another was ordered to maintain a sufficient gate 'with a good catch and latch' for the defence of the town field, and there was a general prohibition on allowing horses, mares or other cattle to graze in either of the town fields, by day or night, 'after the corn is sown until it be gotten out of the fields' other than 'upon his or their own ruled grounds'. In Aldford, a similar court was enforcing maintenance of the boundary to the town fields and appointing 'pinners' to control livestock in areas of common arable, pasture and meadow as late as 1774 (Figure 1).[13] These are fascinating glimpses of practices familiar in 'Champion England' but they only take us so far. There is no sign, for example, that in seventeenth-century Alvanley there was a consistent pattern of crop rotation from one year to the next – no regulation, for example, that the two town fields should alternate in their cropping regimes. Rather, the express permission in 1665 to graze one's beasts in the open fields after corn had been sown, provided that it was in one's own 'ruled ground', hints at that urge to break free from communal obligations which was the drive behind enclosure.

Wherever farming within closes was already familiar, so that the advantages of individualism could be appreciated, such open fields as existed were liable to further erosion. The

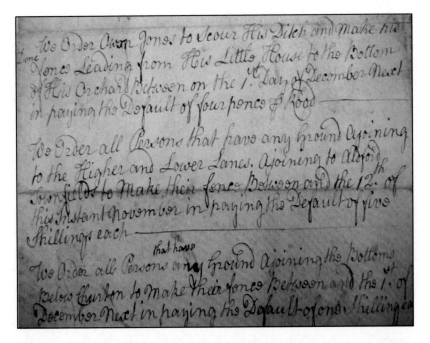

Figure 1. Aldford manor court book, 1774. This extract includes a reference to management of the boundaries of the still-functioning communal town fields.

story, however, can be spun in different ways: stress can be laid either on the precocious enclosure of communally-held land, for which there is evidence as early as the thirteenth century, or on the tenacious survival of small pockets of strips so that they duly appear in the early-Victorian tithe awards and in the case of the open meadow called Wally David (formerly Gwern-y-ddavid) at Shocklach Oviatt persist to this day (Figure 2).[14] The connecting thread is overwhelming reliance on individual initiative as the means by which west Cheshire was enclosed: a process ranging from amicable negotiation to hotly-contested acquisitiveness but a gradual, piecemeal activity stretching over at least seven centuries. So we find, for example, a deliberate policy on the part of St Werburgh's Abbey, Chester during the second half of the thirteenth century to consolidate arable holdings where possible, as at Manley where the abbot acquired from Robert fitz Roger of Manley two and a half selions in *Asponesfurlong* adjacent to other land he already held with the intention of extending a hedge or ditch around them, and at Poulton where he was given three butts by Sir William Lancelyn 'so that the abbot may enclose the said butts and make a grange and cottage'.[15] Similar piecemeal consolidation, though at a humbler level, can be seen at Calveley where by a charter dated 28 May 1346 William de Bulkeley of Alpraham gave to Hugh del Cleyus 'a certain plot of land and waste next to Hugh's hedge' on condition that Hugh and his heirs 'shall dig and make an enclosure between the lands of William and Hugh in perpetuity'.[16] A century and a half later, on 20 December 1491, Jankyn Williamson of Stretton leased to Jankyn Leche of Carden 'certain parcels of ground in Tilston as heretofore been open field' in terms which show that here, too, consolidation and enclosure went together: 'all the Overtywarts flatt shooting afore the gatehouse of the parsonage of Tilston ... one butt cloven in two shooting on the said flatt ... and two other butts shooting on the said flatt next to the hedge of a croft of Randall Carden'.[17]

What appear to be more contentious initiatives came to the county court. In 1282 the pasture between the town fields of Claughton and Oxton was ordered to remain common 'until peace was established between England and Wales', after which the prior of Birkenhead was given permission to have a

Figure 2 (opposite). Wally David (Gwern-y-ddavid) open meadow, Shocklach Oviatt, from the air, 1971. The surviving open meadow still retains a number of 'doles' held by different local farmers, shown by the contrasting 'striped' effect.

reasonable boundary established 'by a perambulation of good and lawful men' for the portion he claimed. Five years later, Robert the rector of Waverton brought a plea against Adam Prachet, who was ordered to remove the hedge he had raised which was preventing the rector from making his furrow straight to the heads of his selions.[18] In 1307–08, there was a dispute over shares in 55 acres of woodland at Aldersey, formerly 'undivided' and held in common but partitioned about fourteen years previously, so that several individuals now claimed to hold distinct portions of 7 or 14 acres each; the jurors were satisfied that there had been common consent to the partition so the various entitlements were confirmed.[19]

The role played by manorial lords in the medieval enclosure movement is best known from the alleged depopulation of rural settlements in the fifteenth and sixteenth centuries, which horrified the likes of Rous and More as noted already and prompted government intervention in an attempt to curtail the practice. In 1517, for example, the king commissioned a series of regional enquiries into all enclosures since Michaelmas 1489 which had led to the demolition of buildings, the conversion of arable to pasture and the creation of parks, with the intention of ordering that all this be reversed under threat of a heavy fine. This commission has yielded some of the best evidence available for the detrimental effects of this change of land use, particularly in 'Champion England' on the clay soils of the midlands where – in an era of reduced population – the great open arable fields and their associated nucleated villages were vulnerable to social and economic forces favouring more pastoral farming. We read, for example, of 'sixty persons ... compelled tearfully to depart' following William Coope's enclosure of the arable and effective destruction of twelve houses in Wormleighton (Warwickshire), and of three ploughs made idle and fifteen people evicted by the prior of St Frideswide at Binsey just outside Oxford, so that they 'led an evil and wretched existence, until life ended.' This simplistic approach is seriously challenged today, with emphasis rightly being placed on a host of other reasons why settlements might become deserted and on the long slow decline of places such as those cited here before there was any lordly intervention to finish them off. However, the immediate question is the relevance of these enquiries to our understanding of enclosure in Cheshire. The answer is that there was very little to report: four enclosures of between one and four acres each in the fields of Chester, and emparking by John Legh at Bagguley, William Troutbeck at Brimstage, Thomas Massey at Puddington and Ralf Egerton at Ridley, involving in any one instance twenty acres of arable at most. In all but one case we are specifically told that there had been no depopulation or destruction of dwellings as a result, the sole exception being in Ridley, where Egerton was reported a year or so before the enquiry to have enclosed and converted to pasture six acres of arable land and one acre of common, leading to the demolition of one cottage. The editor's conclusion from all this, in the published edition of these findings in 1897, was that 'the enclosing movement had made practically no headway' in this region[20] but in fact the reverse was the case: these meagre returns are exactly what we should expect from a county where there was already an abundance of pasture, already plenty of enclosed land, and where the years under scrutiny, 1489–1517, provided no more than a brief snapshot of a process which had been going on for over 200 years.

It was a process which would continue apace. In March 1528, James Huxley of Brindley received a grant of 'two closes of land in Huxley and four butts of land in the fields of Huxley', precisely the picture of open strips mixed with enclosures which Leland was to observe a decade or so later. In February 1643, John Leche of Carden leased to Essex Clarke rector of Tilston various portions of land in Tilston including 'two butts lying all along the hedge on the west side in [Stewes Croft]', another 'two butts lying all along the hedge on its east side', plus 'two lounds of ground nowe enclosed and made into a croft by itself in the township of Horton',[21] all of which again gives an impression of intermingled strips and closes. The same image emerges from early seventeenth-century *Inquisitions Post Mortem*, government enquiries into the holdings of deceased tenants-in-chief of the crown. Here we read, for example, that among the possessions of Robert Brerewood of Chester, who died in May 1601, were '9 loondes in Handbridge in the common fields there containing by estimation 3 Acres ... 7 closes of land in Claverton in Handbridge and a parcel of close in the Croftes and ... 4 parcels called Four Loondes in Handbridge and Claverton in the common fields there'; George Bostock (died November 1620), held among other property 'a close called Cockley Butts with a small part adjoining 20 loonds in the common field of Aldford'.[22]

It would be fair to add, though, that the vast majority of holdings recorded in these seventeenth-century *Inquisitions Post Mortem* seem already to have been entirely enclosed. Being focused on the possessions of the gentry, rather than of smallholders and tenant farmers, they are not fully representative, but it is worth noting that when Celia Fiennes journeyed from Nantwich to Chester in 1698 – commenting, incidentally, on the numerous small cattle herds in the pastures, such that farmers co-operated in milking and cheesemaking – she also observed that 'it's much on enclosures'.[23] By now, although open field strips might survive, in nearly every township the balance of land use was against them. Such was the case for example at Clotton, even though it has abundant evidence of former strips in the present-day landscape in the form of reverse-S field boundaries and the zigzag pattern of roads which previously ran between furlongs; a portion of unenclosed 'town field' also appears on an estate map of 1734 (Figure 3). But an Arderne family rental, unfortunately undated but on the style of handwriting to be assigned to the end of the seventeenth century, suggests that closes – variously described as fields, crofts or meadow – were far more important to the tenants here than their stake in the open field area. Of the nine tenants listed (other than landless cottagers), four seem to have held nothing other than enclosures; of the remainder, one paid a rent of 11 shillings for 'townfield ground' out of a total of £18 12s 8d, another 17s 6d out of £17 7s 6d, another 8 shillings out of £15 8s 2d, another 16 shillings out of £3 4s 0d, and another 8s 6d out of £7 2s 6d. In the adjacent township of Duddon, two tenants paid, respectively, £1 19s 6d for 'townfield ground' out of a total rent of £23 12s 5d, and 7 shillings out of £8 5s 4d; a third had no stake in the town field at all.[24]

Baker and Butlin's *Field Systems of the British Isles*, published in 1973, rightly pointed out that there is plenty of evidence of the continuing enclosure of open fields in Cheshire during the eighteenth century,[25] but this should really be seen as a tidying-up operation covering the remnants which survived. Estate maps produced for the Grosvenor and Egerton families during the 1730s, showing the areas farmed as arable strips and communal meadows and pastures occupying well over half the land surface of townships such as Aldford and Farndon in the Dee valley, give a misleading impression of west Cheshire as a whole, let alone the rest of the county. These were conservatively-run estates, and while we cannot prove that the maps were intended to initiate the process of enclosure

Figure 3. Aerial view of Clotton, 1947, showing the area of the former Town Field. Reverse-S field boundaries and variously-aligned ridge and furrow are indicative of former open field arable, some of which survived into the eighteenth century.

– and we know that the manorial court at Aldford was still dealing with communal farming in the 1770s – the landscape they depict had certainly been replaced by the time of the tithe awards a century later; the sole survivors of the open fields to be shown here were two adjacent half-acre 'quillets in town field' without a hedge between them, duly recorded in Aldford.[26] In the early decades of the eighteenth century, both the Grosvenors and the Egertons were involved with enclosures elsewhere. A map of 1735 shows John Egerton to have been allocated 100 acres of former common pasture at Upton Heath north east of Chester, with a further twelve landowners receiving the remaining eighty-two acres between them.[27] Sir Richard Grosvenor may have been aware of the reorganisation of tenancies and enclosure of the remaining portion of the town field in Chowley, not later than 1727, when the local rector tried to clarify with the Grosvenor agent how their respective entitlements to tithe were affected; eight holdings were involved but as the rector's memorandum puts it 'the particular fields and closes time out of mind held to the said houses are so disposed of and the whole so new modelled that no one tenement is the same as it was before ... the town field which pays tithes in kind, formerly occupied by several persons, is under the present disposition in the tenure of one'.[28]

For their part, eighteenth-century glebe terriers, recording holdings for the support of the parish priest, make some reference to strips in no less than thirty-five parishes well-distributed across the county, but also point to ongoing reorganisation. An example is a terrier for Wallasey dated 8 July 1712 which includes 'a new close with a large headland adjoining called the new Inclosure ... exchanged for some butts in the town field ... now inclosed by [the rector] Mr John Forshall ... containing one acre and a half'.[29] And while the

Figure 4. Ridge and furrow in Tilston's former Town Field. Broad, reverse-S, ridge and furrow survives in the pastures which succeeded an area of open field arable still worked in strips into the eighteenth century. By then, however, piecemeal enclosure was proceeding apace.

great majority of land transfers by this time involved enclosed fields rather than strips, the names given to these closes are sometimes indicative of their former disposition. Thus, a lease to John Simpson of Tilston in February 1731 of 'those closes or parcels of land ... commonly called ... the Long Land in Townfield, the Nearer Land in Town Field, the Further Land in Town Field' plus various surviving butts, implies from the nomenclature that the community's long-established open arable field, still evidenced by reverse-S ridge and furrow to this day, was in the process of being broken up into separate portions (Figure 4).[30] It is also significant that by the early years of the nineteenth century the manorial court at Alvanley, while still serving a useful purpose in enforcing the maintenance of roadways, hedges and ditches, was no longer concerned with the regulation of the town fields, presumably because they no longer existed; instead, it was anxious to prevent trespasses on private property, the jury on 26 December 1803 ordering that 'if any person is seen going over John Atherton's meadow from the green to Joseph Griffith's new hay, to pay the sum of one shilling for each offence, the money to go to the informer'.[31]

If we 'fast forward' to the tithe awards of the early years of Victoria's reign, study of which has been facilitated by Cheshire Record Office's initiative in placing them online, we witness a landscape in which only tiny, isolated pockets of unenclosed strips survived. At Horton, out of fourteen plots variously called 'Town Field', 'Near Town Field' or 'Further Townfield' – an area of about eleven acres in total, clearly taken from the former unenclosed community 'town field' – three were compact enclosures of two to three acres each but the rest unenclosed 'quillets' mostly under half an acre in extent. At Wallasey, fifteen 'lounds' in town field and a further nine 'lounds' in Liscard town field are shown, nearly all less than half an acre in size: all are long narrow unenclosed strips, but among them are two other plots, slightly wider than normal so presumably the product of amalgamation, one unnamed, the other called 'part of town field', which had already been enclosed. At Edge, three unenclosed 'quillets or loons' averaging about half an acre in size sat in the midst of a seven-acre enclosed field called 'Nine Butts', while at Heswall, close to the boundary with Gayton, within a sequence of six consecutive 'quillets', most again about half-an-acre in extent, three at one end are shown as enclosed, the other three as open. Elsewhere, apart from Aldford as noted already, there are examples of single unenclosed quillets surviving, as at Carden and Tilston.[32]

All this should be seen in the context of a parliamentary enclosure movement which, especially in 'champion country', had been in full swing for the past hundred years and had not yet run its course: a total of 2,479 enclosure acts covering open field arable in England were passed by parliament between 1730 and 1844 and the last such enclosure, for Elmstone Hardwicke in Gloucestershire, was not to come until 1914.[33] Within this total there was a solitary example in Cheshire, involving some 126 acres of open arable in St Mary's on the Hill, Chester, enclosed between 1805 and 1807, besides which, in 1784, a further 100 acres or so in the town fields of Frodsham were subject to a formal award drawn up by commissioners appointed without recourse to parliament.[34] The avoidance of parliamentary enclosure did not of course mean that the social consequences associated with it were necessarily averted, still less the legal costs incurred in securing whatever form of agreement was reached along with the expense of hedging, ditching and roadmaking which followed: there were winners and losers in any enclosure, and we can be sure that there would have been a good deal of (rarely recorded) coercion behind some private agreements. But the fees and expenses specific to parliamentary enclosure – which seem to have averaged about £2 per acre in the 'champion' counties in the first half of the nineteenth century – were certainly saved.[35]

Communally-worked meadows, where farmers typically took hay from their own 'doles' before these were thrown open for general grazing, were also enclosed piecemeal, apparently without much difficulty. Grants of individually-held meadows can be found as far back as the thirteenth century, such as the conveyance of a carefully-defined portion of meadow in Blacon by Roger de Mainwaring to Robert fitz Robert, separated by a brook from the abbot of Chester's own meadow and duly recorded in the abbey cartulary.[36] The manorial court rolls of

Ashton in Tarvin (now Ashton Hayes) in 1703 depict a landscape in which the meadows had already been enclosed but there was still some interdependence between neighbours: 'we … enjoin John Pearson to scour his watercourse all along his meadow within this manor a yard broad and a foot deep.'[37] As with open field strips, the early-Victorian tithe awards record a few areas of still-unenclosed meadow persisting alongside already-enclosed neighbours, such as the eight 'quillets in Town Meadow' (plus others with slightly-different names) at Barrow, the three 'quillets in Sellers Meadow' at Cotton Edmunds, and the three 'quillets in Town Meadow' at Newton cum Larton; they also appear under other names in meadows at Bidston, Dodleston, Saughall Massie and Shocklach Oviatt, and in the last case – as noted already – survive to some extent to this day. Overwhelmingly, however, the evidence of the tithe awards is that these meadows had already been enclosed, like the seven portions of 'Town Meadow' in Aldford, the smallest of which was almost an acre in size, the largest upwards of seven acres, evidently the product of the amalgamation of neighbouring doles since most of them were about as wide as they were long.[38] In cases such as these, a memory of common meadows lived on in their names even though they were no longer being managed as such.

Possession of arable strips or of doles in the meadows might be disputed from time to time but the evidence was fairly obvious: the proprietor could be seen working the plots and they could be measured, exchanged, amalgamated and enclosed. By contrast, entitlement to graze animals in common pastures – sometimes called 'wastes' – was less tangible. It was a customary right enjoyed by those with arable strips, sometimes extended to landless cottagers, but unless the resource was under pressure it might not matter precisely how many beasts this meant. It was also very tempting for individuals to encroach on the edges of the commons by enclosing plots without permission, and from medieval times common law protected such encroachments by allowing them to become the occupier's own property if they continued for twenty years without payment of rent. Again, if pasture was plentiful this might well happen, becoming a means by which cottagers acquired portions of land of their own, but as the resource diminished and was eyed as potentially lucrative if put to other uses, the practice came to be seen as a menace. At Ashton in Tarvin during the seventeenth century the manorial court jury was supposed to enquire 'of encroachments upon the lord's waste', whether 'any tenant have inclosed lands accustomed to lie open', and whether 'any tenant hath surcharged the common', articles which hint at the tensions which might arise.[39] Accordingly, the enclosure of common pastures – to which we can add common woodland if also a grazing asset – was often less straightforward than enclosure of well-defined strips of arable or meadow. On the one hand, there was the threat from encroachment if they were left open, on the other the fact that any proposal to apportion plots for enclosure was liable to prompt a host of claims, some of which might be difficult to verify and quantify. All this might lead to conflict and helps to explain why nearly all Cheshire's enclosure awards, whether preceded by an Act or managed through the appointment of commissioners without recourse to parliament, related to this type of land: typically leaving us with the straight-sided, right-angled fields which emerged from surveyors' drawing-boards.

We do, however, need to keep the problems of enclosing the commons in perspective. It was possible to achieve this without any obvious rancour, and certainly without a commissioners' award, especially if only a few claimants were involved. At Burton near Tarvin, for example, a memorandum of agreement with accompanying sketch map, dated 4 November 1780, was sufficient to apportion the eighteen-acre common between three claimants after they had had it surveyed and valued; an apprentice to one of the parties acted as witness to the signatures. It helped here that Burton was a small township without a plethora of landowners – the same families dominated the tithe award to the virtual exclusion of any other owner half-a-century later – and it also helped that a convergence of routeways at the common, like spokes of a wheel, provided a convenient basis for determining the allocations, broadly in keeping with respective liabilities to the land tax. Thus, Captain Beauclerk and his leasehold tenant Pattison Ellams were allocated 'all that part of the said common which lies between the before mentioned road [from Bruen Stapleford to Tarporley] and the road which goes from the Warren house towards Mr Robert Withinshaw's house over the said common containing three statute acres, three roods and twenty-three perches': slightly more than they were entitled to strictly on the basis of land tax contribution but a well-defined, self-contained plot (Plate 6).[40] A little more formally, on 11 October 1727, the four lords of the manor of Utkinton and Willington, Richard and James Arderne, Charles Henchman and John Prescot acting for the chapter of Chester cathedral, all signed an agreement to divide into six shares 'in order to be inclosed' a previously-demarcated portion of the commons, and to have it immediately bounded by an outer ring hedge; they also agreed to maintain their respective parts of this ring hedge and to assist one another in combating any attempt to dispute their right to the enclosure or to break down the hedge.[41] Even more formal was the decision of John Stanley Massey of Puddington Hall to have the indentures he had agreed on 4 and 5 September 1772 with the feoffees of Whitchurch School for the

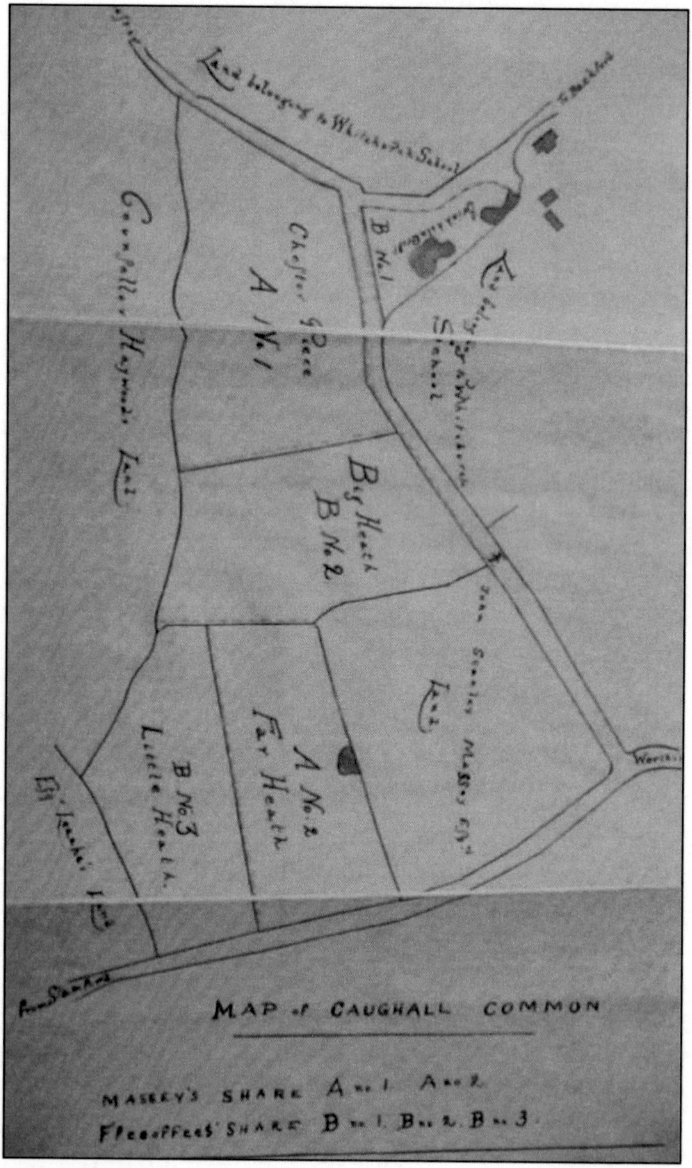

Figure 5. Caughall Common enclosure map, 1772. This map accompanied an award covering just under fifty acres, achieved by agreement between the two proprietors involved.

Figure 6. Caughall Common, 2011. The plot shown as 'Chester Piece' in Figure 5 is on the right and Chester Zoo now occupies the area to the left.

enclosure of equal portions of Caughall common enrolled in Chancery; these were the only parties involved and they each took 24 acres 25 perches, accepting also an equal share of the costs of maintaining the roads (Figures 5, 6).[42]

With varying degrees of assertiveness, this must have happened time and again, leaving enclosure by commissioners' award – for which we have around a hundred examples in Cheshire beginning with Cuddington in 1767 and ending with Runcorn and Weston in 1898 – a relatively-minor contributor to the process overall, albeit considerably more significant than it was for open field arable. A little over half these awards, some fifty-four, were the result of Acts of Parliament – parliamentary enclosure strictly defined – covering 27,000 acres of 'commons and wastes', some 3.8% of the county's total landed area but still a lower percentage than for any neighbouring county. Over the country as a whole, parliamentary enclosure of commons and wastes, stimulated by a sense that these tracts of countryside could be put to better use during the Napoleonic Wars, peaked in the first two decades of the nineteenth century, when almost half of all the acts passed between 1730 and 1845 went through. As the first President of the Board of Agriculture Sir John Sinclair said in 1803, 'we have begun another campaign against the foreign enemies of the country ... let us not be satisfied with the liberation of Egypt or the subjugation of Malta, but let us subdue Finchley Common, let us conquer Hounslow Heath'.[43] By then, however, most of Cheshire's commons and wastes had, from Sinclair's perspective, long been forced into submission.

Estate papers give us several glimpses of the trouble which the enclosure of commons might cause, even when tiny amounts were involved. There was lengthy correspondence, for example, between Jonathan Bruen of Stapleford and John Crewe, chief forester of Delamere, between 1668 and 1670 over an encroachment at Kelsborrow variously claimed to be either one-and-a-half acres or four acres in extent, where Bruen admitted that he had built a cottage but only 'out of charity for a poor man ... to get bread' and which he felt 'might have been connived at'. Instead, Crewe had gone to the lengths of getting authorisation from the Duke of Newcastle, justice in eyre of all the king's forests north of the Trent, to have the enclosure and cottage pulled down. The case also went to the Solicitor-General after Bruen complained about the keeper who carried out the order, and to the local JPs who had to take legal opinion on the parish responsible for giving poor relief to the evicted man and his family, since the plot where he had been living was extra-parochial.[44] It was the proliferation of cases such as this, allied to the need to protect the crown's interests against further erosion, which led ultimately to the enclosure of Delamere Forest by Act of Parliament in the early nineteenth century – although such were the complexities of the claims to common rights lodged by landholders from neighbouring townships that it was necessary to pass three successive acts, in 1812, 1814 and 1818, and to draw up three successive awards, dated 31 December 1816, 1 October 1817 and 17 December 1819, before everything was settled. The king took half the unenclosed forest by value, some 3,847 acres (slightly more than half by area) to be administered by the Surveyor General of Woods and Forests mostly as timber plantations, with the remainder being allocated for enclosure by those whose rights were upheld.[45] The distinctive landscape to the east of Kelsall, with its straight roads and straight-sided fields interspersed with older enclosures such as the Old and New Pales, was the result.

In similar vein, on 27 December 1799 James Hassall wrote to John Arden, the principal lord of the manor, complaining about 'the daily encroachments which takes [sic] place on Clotton commons', which threatened if the plots were built upon not only to 'overrun as it were the common but fill the town full of poor'. This had been going on for several decades; an account dated 27 August 1753 of 'cottages and inclosures … erected or inclosed within twenty years last past and for which no leases have been taken or chief rents yet paid' listed eight such encroachments in Clotton (with a further nine in neighbouring Duddon) such as 'a quarter of an acre about two years ago' on which John Roberts, wheelwright, had erected 'a building or shop'. Hassall had only bought his quarter-share of the lordship of Clotton in 1798, but now he recommended to

Figure 7. Clotton Common, 2011. The straight roads and hedges, with right-angled corners to the fields, survive from the formal enclosure of Clotton common in 1816. See also Plate 7.

Arden a 'genearl inclosuering' [*sic*] of the common, threatening to measure up and enclose his own entitlement independently if his proposal came to nought. The upshot was articles of agreement dated 5 January 1805 among the lords of the manor and freeholders of Clotton to proceed to the appointment of commissioners who would make allotments 'in proportion to our freeholds within the same manor', although it was not until 25 January 1816 that the award was eventually made, the opportunity being taken to enclose the adjoining Duddon common as well and to define the township boundary between the two.[46] The enrolling of the award in Chancery gave it the status of a parliamentary enclosure, although this was another example of parliament's involvement – and the expense that incurred – having been avoided (Plate 6 and Figure 7).

Given the disparate nature of the evidence, there are limits to what can be said about the volume of land enclosed at any time. Thomas Wedge's *General View of the Agriculture of the County Palatine of Chester*, published in 1794, estimated there to be 'probably not so much as 1,000 acres' of what he called 'common fields' – that is open arable – left in Cheshire by then. Two generations later, to judge by the tithe awards, those surviving 'quillets' being treated as arable, not all of which were still unenclosed, amounted to eighty acres at most, nearly all in the west of the county. As for remaining 'wastelands, heaths, commons, greens', Wedge suggested 30,000 acres for Cheshire as a whole, compared to just under 200,000 acres estimated by the *New Historical Atlas of Cheshire* for the first half of the seventeenth century on the basis of the *Inquisitions Post Mortem*.[47] At a local level, it is fair to say that final enclosure tended to be delayed where a large number of landowners was involved, so making the process of piecemeal negotiation more protracted. It is no coincidence that townships with the best evidence of surviving unenclosed strips in the tithe awards had a pattern of highly fragmented landownership recorded in those awards: thirty-four different owners in Horton, for example, thirty-two in Heswall, over eighty in Wallasey. Those parishes where recourse was had to a formal award in order to enclose the remaining open field arable, Frodsham and Chester St Mary's, each had a hundred or so different landowners entered in their tithe awards – rather more in the first case, just under in the second; within the enclosure awards themselves, twenty-three and seventeen proprietors respectively received allocations. All this can be contrasted with the picture presented at townships such as Churton Heath, Cotton Abbotts, Lea Newbold and Stretton near Tilston, where settlement today is confined to isolated pockets and neither the shapes nor the names of fields as recorded therein – save possibly for some 'allotments' in Stretton – give any hint that they were once farmed as open arable or common pasture; in these places, landownership as recorded in the tithe awards was either in single hands or in no more than four, and where there was more than one owner at least 80% of the landed area was within the same estate.[48] In these townships, if there had ever been any communal farming, it looks to have been eradicated through enclosure led by a dominant landowner at an early stage, perhaps no later than the sixteenth or seventeenth century, leaving scarcely any documentary or landscape evidence other than some traces of ridge and furrow which it would be unwise to assume without corroboration is the product of open field farming. We have a glimpse of the process at Stretton, where on 20 January 1602 – doubtless in return for some unrecorded inducement – two local gentry who clearly had rights to the common, Owen Stockton of Cuddington and William Batho of Duckington, released all their claims therein to the principal lord, Richard Wright of Bickley 'so that we and the heirs of us ... be clearly barred and excluded from the same for ever'.[49] It might be added, here, that all this has implications for our understanding of the contrasts between 'open' and 'closed' townships, for by any definition Stretton was 'closed' while neighbouring Tilston, with forty-three different landowners and a surviving 'quillet' recorded in the tithe award, was 'open'. The different enclosure experiences in 'open' and 'closed' contexts would repay further study.[50]

There is, however, more to the story, for open arable and unenclosed commons certainly persisted in some places where one or more powerful individuals might have been expected to hasten their demise. The Grosvenor family, for example, owned the bulk of Aldford, the Arderne family nearly all of Alvanley, but as we have seen they both allowed open field farming to continue well into the eighteenth century. Among the awards securing the enclosure of commons, that for Thurstaston was one of the last in the whole of Cheshire, finally deposited with the clerk of the peace in January 1884, yet here there were only four proprietors to whom allotments had to be made, other than Birkenhead Corporation and Thurstaston parish which were assigned a 'Recreation Ground' on Thurstaston Hill on condition that it did not cause a nuisance. So we cannot be too deterministic in our analysis of the factors which prompted or delayed enclosure: all sorts of local circumstances, including petty rivalries and sheer inertia, might have affected the timing. In this connection, it may be significant that some geographical patterns are apparent in the dating of enclosure awards: Waverton's commons were enclosed in 1791, Christleton's in 1794, Tarvin's in 1795, with the initiating Acts of Parliament or private articles of agreement all falling between 1788 and 1791; those of Helsby in 1797, Dunham on the Hill in 1801, Alvanley in 1805, with the relevant acts or articles all between 1792 and 1799; Little Neston's in 1808, Thornton Hough's in 1815, Burton in Wirral's in 1817, all formally initiated between 1799 and 1811.[51] Two of these townships, Dunham and Little Neston, had the same lord of the manor, the earl of Shrewsbury, which probably explains why the articles of agreement to proceed with the enclosure of their commons had identical dates, 31 December 1799: one can imagine him with glass in hand as midnight struck, toasting the arrival of the 1800s with a promise of agricultural improvement. Otherwise, there are no major overlaps in landownership within these sequences and while they could be matters of coincidence the timings may well be the result of a spirit of emulation: effectively that of 'keeping up with the neighbours'. Scholars interested in the advance of open field farming have recently been arguing that between the tenth and the twelfth centuries it spread from one township to another, especially within 'Champion England', precisely in this way, through copying what had been observed to work well for the settlement down the road.[52] In the very different circumstances of the eighteenth and nineteenth centuries, in a part of the country conventionally seen as lying outside the 'champion' zone, we seem to have similar motivations working to put the process into reverse.

References

1. *Leland's Itinerary in England and Wales*, ed. L. Toulmin-Smith (Harvard, 1964), III, 74; IV, 10.
2. B.K. Roberts and S. Wrathmell, *An Atlas of Rural Settlement in England* (2nd edn, London, 2003); S. Rippon, *Beyond the Medieval Village* (Oxford, 2008), 5, 138–49.
3. W. Harrison, *Description of England*, ed. G. Edelen (Ithaca, New York, 1968), 216.
4. Harrison, *Description*, 217.
5. Roberts and Wrathmell, *Atlas of Rural Settlement*, 54.
6. *Leland's Itinerary*, IV, 3.
7. As stressed in Rippon, *Beyond the Medieval Village*, 1–7, 27, 267.
8. Quotation from the preamble to the 'Act for better Cultivation, Improvement and Regulation of the Common Arable Fields, Wastes and Commons of Pasture in this Kingdom', 13 Geo.III, c.81 (1773).
9. C. Dyer, 'Conflict in the landscape: the enclosure movement in England, 1220–1349', *Landscape History*, XXVIII (2006), 21–33; cf. for the wider chronological context R.J.P. Kain, J. Chapman and R.R. Oliver, *The Enclosure Maps*

of England and Wales, 1595–1918 (Cambridge, 2004), e.g. 1–21.

10. V. Chapman, 'Open fields in west Cheshire', *THSLC*, CIV (1953), 35–59; D. Sylvester, 'The open fields of Cheshire', *THSLC*, CVIII (1957), 1–33; D. Sylvester, *The Rural Landscape of the Welsh Borderland* (London, 1969), 267–70; G. Elliott, 'Field systems of north-west England', in A.R.H. Baker and R.A. Butlin, eds, *Field Systems in the British Isles* (Cambridge, 1973), 42–47; G.J. White, 'Open fields and rural settlement in medieval west Cheshire' in T. Scott and P. Starkey, eds, *The Middle Ages in the North-West* (Oxford, 1995), 15–35; P.M. Vipond, 'The Landscape and Settlement of South West Cheshire' (University of Liverpool PhD thesis, 2000). See also 'Selected field-names of Cheshire and its borders' by the CSLH Field-Names Research Group later in this volume.

11. A.D.M. Phillips and C.B. Phillips, *A New Historical Atlas of Cheshire* (Chester, 2002), 52–53.

12. D. Sylvester, 'A note on three-course arable systems in Cheshire', *THSLC*, CX (1959), 183–86.

13. Barnston family deeds: CALS: DBA 15; Aldersey family deeds: CALS: DAL 177; Alvanley manor court records: CALS: DAR A/32, DAR I/3; Aldford manor court records: CALS: DDX 27/2. On the distribution of strips in a repetitive sequence, see, for example, B.K. Roberts, *Landscapes, Documents and Maps* (Oxford, 2008), 82–87, 248–51.

14. White, 'Open fields and rural settlement', 17.

15. *Chartulary or Register of Chester Abbey*, ed. J. Tait (Chetham Soc., 1920–23), I, no. 387, II, no. 718; H.L. Gray, *English Field Systems* (reptd, London, 1969), 253–58.

16. CALS: DAL 429; G.C.O. Bridgeman, *Family of Aldersey* (London, 1899), no. 425.

17. Leche family deeds: CALS: DLE 47.
18. *Chester County Court Rolls*, ed. R. Stewart-Brown (Chetham Soc., 1925), 53, 70.
19. Bridgeman, *Family of Aldersey*, no. 3.
20. *Domesday of Inclosures, 1517–1518*, ed. I. S. Leadam (London 1897), I, 387; II, 403–4, 640–44.
21. Bridgeman, *Family of Aldersey*, no. 379; CALS: DLE 47.
22. *Cheshire Inquisitions Post Mortem, 1603–1660*, ed. R. Stewart-Brown (RSLC, 1934–38), I, 49, 76, cf. 56.
23. *The Journeys of Celia Fiennes*, ed. C. Morris (London, 1947), 177.
24. CALS: DDX 573/1; Arderne family papers: CALS: DAR B/8 pt. 2.
25. Elliott, 'Field systems', 77, 88–92.
26. Eaton Estate MSS maps and plans no. 11 ('a map of part of … Aldford … 1738'); CALS: DEO 1/9 ('map of Crew and Farndon tenements, 1735'); EDT 9 (Aldford tithe award).
27. Phillips and Phillips, *New Historical Atlas*, 54–55.
28. Memo concerning tithe payments in Chowley: CALS: EDD 6/7/1.
29. Wallasey glebe terriers: CALS: EDV 8/90a/6.
30. Tyrwhitt-Drake family deeds: CALS: DTD 34/8.
31. Alvanley manor court records: CALS: DAR G/17.
32. Tithe Awards: CALS: EDT 87 (Carden), 152 (Edge), 199 (Heswall), 208 (Horton), 395 (Tilston), 411 (Wallasey).
33. M. Turner, *English Parliamentary Enclosure* (Folkestone, 1980), 66–71, 211.
34. CALS: QDE 2/4 (Frodsham town fields etc., quantity converted from Cheshire acres shown therein), 2/13 (Chester St Mary's).
35. M. Turner, *Enclosures in Britain, 1750–1830* (London 1984), 57, 62: approximate figure arrived at by counting Turner's

'physical costs' necessary in any enclosure as one-third and deducting these from his total costs.

36. *Chartulary of Chester Abbey*, II, no. 862.
37. Ashton in Tarvin manor court records: CALS: DDX 27/5.
38. CALS: EDT 9 (Aldford), 37 (Barrow), 47 (Bidston, Saughall Massie), 127 (Cotton Edmunds), 140 (Dodleston), 298 (Newton cum Larton), 355 (Shocklach Oviatt).
39. CALS: DDX 27/29.
40. Baker-Wilbraham family deeds: CALS: DBW M/M/E no. 4
41. CALS: DAR A/52/1.
42. CALS: QDE 2/1.
43. Turner, *English Parliamentary Enclosure*, 178–81.
44. CALS: DAR A/48.
45. *VCH Ches*, II, 172–78.
46. CALS: DAR A 30/2; QDE 1/22.
47. T. Wedge, *General View of the Agriculture of the County Palatine of Chester* (1794), 8; Phillips and Phillips, *New Historical Atlas*, 54.
48. CALS: EDT 96 (Chester St Mary's), 113 (Churton Heath), 127 (Cotton Abbotts), 163 (Frodsham), 199 (Heswall), 208 (Horton), 231 (Lea Newbold), 377 (Stretton), 411 (Wallasey); QDE 2/4 (Frodsham town fields etc.), 2/13 (Chester St Mary's). Churton Heath and Cotton Abbotts were in single ownership, Lea Newbold had two owners (with nearly 90% in the hands of Joseph White), Stretton four (with over 80% belonging to John Hurleston Leche).
49. CALS: DLE 30.
50. For an excellent discussion of 'open' and 'closed' townships, see P. Bird, 'Landownership and Settlement Change in South-West Cheshire from 1750 to 2000' (University of Liverpool PhD thesis, 2007), 67–83.

51. CALS: QDE 1/8 (Christleton), 1/9 (Tarvin and Mouldsworth), 1/11 (Frodsham Lordship and Helsby), 1/12 (Dunham on the Hill), 1/15 (Little Neston), 1/20 (Leighton and Thornton Hough), 1/24 (Burton in Wirral), 1/49 (Thurstaston), 2/5 (Waverton), 2/11 (Alvanley).
52. B.K. Roberts and S. Wrathmell, *Region and Place* (London, 2002), 18-24, 72-77, 143; Rippon, *Beyond the Medieval Village*, 17-19.

5

A DESCRIPTION AND HISTORY OF WALK MILL
ON THE RIVER GOWY IN FOULK STAPLEFORD

John Whittle

Introduction

Walk Mill is located in the west of the old Palatine of Cheshire now known as 'Cheshire West and Chester'. It is about eight kilometres east-south-east of the centre of Chester and lies between the A41 and A51 roads. Geographically, the Clwydian hills of Wales lie to the west and the mid-Cheshire ridge to the east. This includes Beeston surmounted by its well-known castle, whilst to the north the River Mersey flows into the Irish Sea. The county of Shropshire lies to the south of this area with little immediate change in the landscape. The underlying ground is sandstone and this is covered with boulder clay, to a considerable depth in some places, with pockets of gravel and sand, produced by glacial deposits. Historically the main lines of communication have been south to Shrewsbury and, in Roman times, Wroxeter. The routes to Nantwich and London to the south east run through the 'Beeston Gap', a break in the sandstone ridge. The routes to Wirral, North Wales and, eventually, to Ireland pass through Chester.

The area is drained by the River Gowy, which flows northwards from its source just south of Beeston to the River Mersey (Figure 1). It is along the course of this relatively small river and its several tributaries that numerous individual water mills have existed since at least the time of Domesday. The level area surrounding the river hereabouts is a flood plain and

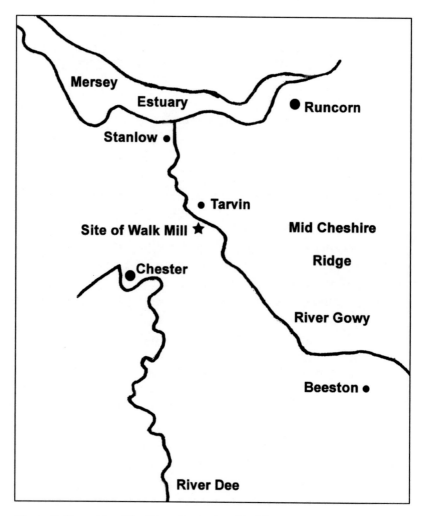

Figure 1. The route of the River Gowy from Peckforton to the Mersey.

water meadows are a feature of the landscape. This part of Cheshire is dominated by pasture, suitable for grazing cows and producing milk and cheese. However, the existence of these mills, and the much larger ones on the River Dee in Chester which were primarily for grinding corn, is evidence that at one time much of the land was arable.[1] It is also interesting to note in this context that since at least 1580 the motifs for Chester and Cheshire have featured corn sheaves.

Early History
The earliest indication of man in the area surrounding Walk Mill was the discovery of several mesolithic flints which were found in Bruen Stapleford. The earliest known artefact of the Neolithic era is a stone or celt, found in nearby Hargrave in 1901. A domestic settlement consisting of six structures identified by circular drip gullies was discovered in 2001 along the route of a new gas pipeline through Bruen Stapleford.[2] Of these, five were round houses and one was described as 'a bow-sided or oval round house'.[3] A small quantity of pottery was recovered and this has been identified as late Bronze Age. Other pottery finds are probably middle Iron Age. Radio carbon dating indicates that the site was occupied from about 1320 BC to about 150 BC and possibly up to the time of the Roman invasion. Chester (Deva) was a major Roman settlement so it is not surprising that several Roman coins have also been found in this area. A more recent find, in 1997, in a field close to Walk Mill, was a silver coin hoard which dates back to AD 959–75.[4] A major find in November 2004 in a field on the same side of the River Gowy was a hoard of twenty-two silver objects, misnamed the Huxley Hoard (Figure 2), which also date back to the tenth century.[5] It is becoming clear from these finds on both sides of the river that this area of the Gowy valley has been the scene of human activity for longer than previously thought.

Figure 2. The Huxley Hoard showing twenty flattened silver arm rings.

Documentary Evidence

Walk Mill is situated in the parish of Foulk Stapleford, formerly part of the larger parish of Tarvin. The name Stapleford originates from a river crossing, 'ford', and *stapol*, a pillar. Hence a ford marked by a pillar. The first known written use of the name Stapleford is in Domesday Book of 1086 and it appears later in various spellings. The ford, across the River Gowy, was for many years a cart or carriage track between Chester and Nantwich. Ford bridge now carries an unclassified road over the Gowy. An alternative crossing, suitable for pack horses, known locally as the 'Roman Bridges', still exists about a kilometre downstream.

The road leading down to the river is known as Guy Lane, a possible corruption of Gowy, which may itself be derived from the Welsh 'gwy' meaning water as in Afon Gwy (River Wye). In the seventh century the Gowy may have been a boundary between the Welsh and the Anglo-Saxons. Indeed the name of Tarvin has been interpreted as being derived from the Welsh 'tervyn' meaning 'boundary'.

In Domesday Book Stapleford is mentioned as being held by Ralph Venator (elsewhere Ralph Hunter) from Earl Hugh. The entry continues:

Wulfsi held it; he was a free man.
2 hides paying tax. Land for 3 ploughs. In lordship 1;
1 rider, 2 villagers and 5 smallholders with 3 ploughs.
Woodland 2 acres long and 1 wide; a mill.
The value was and is 16 shillings. [6]

This is the earliest known reference to a mill in Stapleford and it is reasonable to assume that it was located on the River Gowy, although no clear position can be designated. However, it must have been a corn mill as fulling mills were only introduced into

139

England in the late twelfth century.[7] Eighteen corn mill sites were described by the Domesday surveyors in Cheshire.[8] This has led Bott to estimate that there were less than two mills per 100 square miles in Cheshire, compared with more southern counties such as Dorset and Wiltshire which had in excess of twenty-eight.[9] The name 'Walk Mill' itself implies a fulling mill since the name originates from the method by which the material was fulled even before water mills were used. This involved treading the material underfoot whereas waterwheels used hammers to beat the cloth instead.

Stapleford was divided into two manors in the thirteenth century; one part, nearer Tarvin, became Bruen Stapleford, after a family who owned lands locally. The other part of Stapleford took the name Foulk, after Fulc de Orreby, justiciar of Chester (1259–60), who in 1243 and 1260 was recorded as holding half of Stapleford: 'Fulco's moiety of Stapleford'.

One piece of evidence for an early fulling mill in this area comes from Duddon. In 1357 in the Cheshire Forest Eyre there is reference to the pleas or accusations submitted by the foresters, riders and regarders that 'they presented 10 years ago (1347) William de Pryers built in Duddon a fulling mill which is to harm the beasts. And it is worth 3s 4d for which William will answer and it is to be destroyed and forfeit made to the lord'.[10] There were ninety-nine corn mills in Cheshire between 1287 and 1386[11] rising to at least 203 by 1485.[12]

In the early sixteenth century there is a reference to Hockenhull Mill, believed originally to be on the site of Stapleford Mill.[13] However, by the seventeenth century documentary references are more numerous. In 1607 two mills at Stapleford were reported to be out of action because the River Gowy froze up.[14] And by the later seventeenth century there are numerous references to the mill. An indenture of 16 July 1686–87, now lost, refers to the 'Walkemilne buildings and

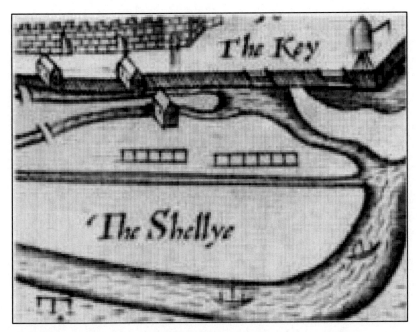

Figure 3. Detail from Speed's map of Exeter, showing tenter frames next to a fulling mill. Celia Fiennes may have seen something similar on her visit to Exeter.

tenter thereunto' which belonged to John Bruen. Further references include a marriage settlement, dated 1 April 1692, between John Bruen of Bruen Stapleford and Honor Winnington which mentions 'messuages or tenements and Walkemill or Fulling mill in Fulke Stapleford with lands and tenements thereto belonging in possession of John Burscough. Clerk, at £4 p.a.'[15] This is followed by an indenture dated 12 November 1692 between John Burscough of Stoke next Guldeford (Guildford) in the County of Surrey clerke (clerk) on the one part and Sarah Barlett of the City of Chester widow, in which there is mention of 'the tentre yard'.[16] This is an important reference because a tentor or tenter was a place

141

where treated cloth was hung out to dry and bleach, indicating that it was located close to Walk Mill and is further evidence of the function of the mill at that time. A section of Speed's map of Exeter, dating to 1611, shown in Figure 3, depicts two sets of tenter frames next to a fulling mill. The following extract from Celia Fiennes's diary, written in 1698, whilst she was in Exeter, during a tour from Bristol to Plymouth, gives a good description of the processes that would have taken place:

> ... then they lay them [rolls of serge] in soack in vrine then they soape them and soe put them into the fulling-mills and soe worke them in the mills drye till they are thick enough, then they turne water into them and so scower them; the mill does draw out and gather in the serges, its a pretty divertion to see it, a sort of huge notch'd timbers like great teeth, one would thinke it should injure the serges but it does not, the mills draws in with such a great violence that if one stands neere it, and it catch a bitt of your garments it would be ready to draw in the person even in a trice; when they are thus scour'd they drye them in racks strained out, which are as thick set one by another as will permitt the dresser to pass between, and huge large fields occupy'd this way almost all round the town which is to the river side.[17]

Further references to the mill occur in 1703 when 'Walk milne buildings and Tenters' and other fields were leased by Jonathan Bruen to John Waine, yeoman, of Foulk Stapleford. These fields included the 'Tentre yard'.[18]

From the early eighteenth century there are a series of documents which show that there was a close relationship between John Waine, John Beard (fuller), Robert Withinshaw (dyer) and Robert's son Richard, who was married to Waine's daughter, Marjorie. All this was linked to business interests and land transactions in the vicinity of Walk Mill. There is for example an indenture dated 25 March 1721 'between John Beard of Tarvin in the County of Chester, Fuller, of the one part and Robert Withershaw of Foulk Stapleford in the County of Chester, Dyer, of other part.'[19] As there are no other known fulling mills in the area it can be safely assumed that Beard fulled cloth at Walk Mill. His widow, Abigail, is given as living in Greenlooms, Warton (Waverton). There is also a receipt (or settlement) dated 15 March 1727 which is shown in Figure 4. The text reads:

> Refund of John Waine the sum of one pound seven(teen) shillings and sixpence being in full for milling cloth by farthing pots for Robert Withershaw and likewise for all accounts betwixt Robert Withershaw and farthing pots and Ralph Done of Tarvin as witness our hands. Farthing Pots his mark.
> Witness Edward Royle, Ralph Done.[20]

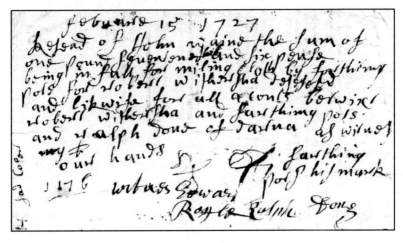

Figure 4. Copy of receipt for milling cloth by Farthing Pots.

In an Indenture Tripartite dated 20 December 1727 Moses Gill, an Administrator of John Beard's will, is described as late of Tarvin, fuller, deceased.[21] Again, like Beard it can be safely assumed that he was the fuller at Walk Mill. He left a will, which is now lost, but the administration document for Gill is still extant.[22] Then in his will of 1728 John Waine left the tenements called Walk Mill Tentre, Dones Meadow and Burtons Croft to his daughter Marjorie Withinshaw.[23] (The receipt, above, suggests that Marjorie's husband, John Waine's son-in-law, had died earlier.)

In 1802 Randle Wilbraham leased to John Dutton, farmer, and Thomas Howell, miller, both of Bruen Stapleford, the site of a water mill called Walk Mill with pools, races and dams in the Township of Foulke Stapleford. This was now in the tenure of Margaret Bennett and amounted to 1 acre 2 roods 11 perches of arable land and 30 perches of water and waste at a rent of £15 15s 0d. This lease was for the lives of Randle Wilbraham, John Dutton, son of said John Dutton and Thomas Howell, provided that Dutton and Howell erected a new water corn mill within three years upon the pools and race and maintained it once erected. Although there is no further evidence to substantiate this claim, it is possible that the change from a fulling mill to a flour mill occurred at this time. [24]

In his will of 1815, Richard Howell, a yeoman of Greenlooms in Tarvin, bequeathed 'all messages, mills and lands which I hold by virtue of one or more leases unto my son, Joseph Howells'.[25] By the early 1820s ministers from the Primitive Methodists, Chester Circuit attended 'Walk Mills' [sic] on Sundays at least once per month; '... there were others of influence, such as Mr Dean of Walk Mills and Warburton of Burton Hall, who opened their houses for preaching, and extended hospitality to the preachers'.[26] By 1841 Robert Phoenix

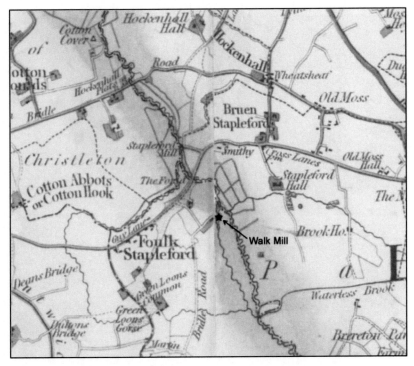

Figure 5. Bryant's map showing the location of Walk Mill.

is given as miller. All subsequent owners and occupiers of the mill can thereafter be found in the census returns.

The first map to depict Walk Mill is Bryant's map of Cheshire dating to 1831. This names Stapleford Mill and shows the position of Walk Mill (depicted as a star in Figure 5). However, by 1842 the first edition OS map names both mills. From Bryant's map it appears that the River Gowy divided into two at the junction with a tributary called Waterless Brook. The more easterly of these rivers meandered through the flood plain and constituted the boundary of Foulk Stapleford. The westerly branch meandered to Walk Mill. Both branches merged

145

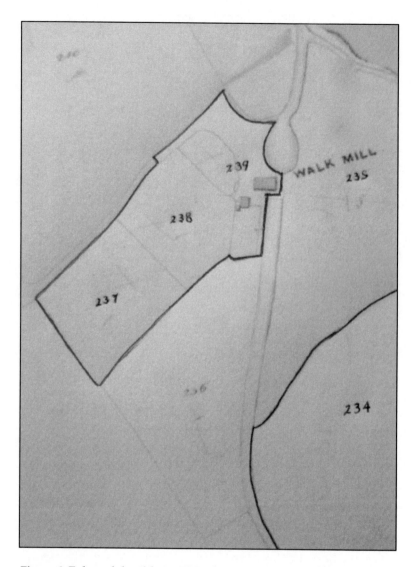

Figure 6. Enlarged detail from 1838 tithe map of Foulk Stapleford (CALS: EDT 160/2) showing fields and mill occupied by R. Phoenix and also Sintry (Tintry) meadow (234).

together again on the north side of the mill after an apparent pond, which was probably formed by the turbulent water from the tail-race. An earlier map of Cheshire, surveyed by Burdett and dating to 1777, shows 156 watermills in Cheshire. However, Burdett's map fails to show Walk Mill, although Stapleford Mill is shown.[27]

The 1838 tithe map indicates that the river leading to Walk Mill had been straightened. Figure 6 shows the mill and the surrounding fields. Plots 237, 238 and 239 were owned by Randle Wilbraham and occupied by Robert Phoenix. Field number 234 on the opposite side of the River Gowy to Walk Mill was called Tintry (mis-transcribed in the tithe apportionment as Sintry meadow).[28] It seems likely that this is probably the same, or an adjacent field, with a slightly corrupted name, referred to in the above indentures of 100 years previously as tenter or Tentre yard. If so, this shows the likely location of the tenter frames where, after treatment in the mill, the cloth was hung out to dry and bleach and to be shaped.

By 1875 the OS map names the straightened section of the river leading to the mill as the Mill Race. This suggests that the straightening of the river had been carried out to ensure an uninterrupted flow of water to the mill. Further straightening of the river's course was undertaken during the Second World War by Italian prisoners of war. Figure 7, taken in 1947, shows the course of the straightened river at Walk Mill. Other photographs in the same series reveal that the straightening and clearing process took place both upstream and downstream of the mill.

The mill is presumed to have ceased being a corn mill during the First World War and was subsequently used as a dwelling (Figure 8). During the Second World War the

147

Figure 7. Aerial view of River Gowy near Walk Mill, 1947, showing a moated site. Note the spoil from the straightening of the river which shows as a light area.

metalwork was removed for scrap and the building was used for storage. In 1965, J. Harold Norris noted that 'the three storey brick and slate mill and house [was] used up to 1960. Mill portion roofless and house in not much better condition. Both buildings now used as hay stores'.[29] Evidence from local residents suggests that the building was demolished by the owner in 1960 due to the building's misuse.

An aerial photograph of the site of Walk Mill in 1983 taken by Rhys Williams clearly shows a moated site on the opposite side of the River Gowy. The history of this site is not known although there are many conjectures as to its origins.[30]

Reconstruction
The mill site and the adjacent land were owned by several local people during the latter part of the twentieth century. In 1999 Mr Ben Jones purchased 200 acres of land in Foulk Stapleford including the site of Walk Mill. Planning permission was obtained in 2006 and work started on reconstructing the mill building soon afterwards. During the course of the preparation work, an archaeological survey was carried out.[31] The survey found that the floor plan of the previous mill survived and excavations were carried out to expose the foundations of the mill to ensure their structural integrity and to underpin where necessary. The reconstruction work thus took place on the footprint of the previous building using old photographs as a guide. The surviving mill structure was constructed of red brick in English Garden Bond with a hard grey mortar. Along its eastern edge the surviving floor plan showed the mill to be constructed of large ashlar sandstone blocks (Figure 9). This would have been to support the weight of the mill wheel and its mechanism, and to protect the mill from the river.

Figure 8. Walk Mill before demolition. (Precise date unknown, but pre-1960.)

Figure 9. Detail of foundations showing sandstone blocks on the wheel side. Note also the old mill grindstone discovered on the site.

In the course of work on the mill site a grinding stone was uncovered. The sack hoist, just discernible in the old photograph, was found and incorporated into the building. As the positions of doorways and fireplaces were revealed during the excavations the interior design also followed as closely as possible that of the previous mill. Recovered materials, such as the floor tiles and hand-made Cheshire bricks, found under the tiles, were used where possible. Some of the installed mechanism was obtained from other disused mill sites, other parts were newly made. The damsel, used for feeding the corn to the grindstones, is original and was found on the site. Oak beams and timber was used throughout. Additionally a date stone engraved 'RW 1668' was found on site. At the time of writing, research has been unable to link this piece of evidence to a particular individual. Nevertheless, the stone has been incorporated above the fireplace in the miller's kitchen.

Plate 8 shows the completed building. Milling restarted in 2008 and Ben Jones, who along with his family developed this project, now produces up to a ton of stoneground wholemeal, white and malted flour a day from wheat grown in the surrounding fields. The flour is used in the miller's kitchen and the surplus is sold to local hotels. Ben Jones has given Walk Mill a new lease of life: a piece of living landscape history in the heart of west Cheshire.

References

1. P. Booth, 'Grain and cereal crops in fourteenth-century Cheshire', talk given as part of Cheshire History Day, 30 October 2010.

2. N. Fairburn et al., 'Brook house farm, Bruen Stapleford. Excavation of a first millennium BC settlement', *JCAS*, LXXVII (2002), 9.

3. Fairburn, 'Brook house farm', 12.

4. J. Whittle, ed., *A History of Hargrave and Huxley* (2nd edn, Hargrave, 2008).

5. J. Graham-Campell and R. Philpott, eds, *The Huxley Viking Hoard* (National Museum of Liverpool, 2009).

6. *Domesday Book: Cheshire*, ed. P. Morgan (Chichester, 1978).

7. 'Fulling mills of the Isle of Wight', Industrial Archaeology Society (2002) <<http://www.iwias.org.uk>>.

8. O.J.P. Bott, 'Cornmill sites in Cheshire', *Ches.Hist.*, XI (1983), 52; but see also X (1982), 53–74; XI (1983), 52–65; XIII (1984), 33–38; XIV (1984), 29–36; XV (1985), 38–42; XVI (1985), 26–33; XVII (1986), 27–33.

9. Bott, 'Cornmill sites', X, 63.
10. Cheshire Forest Eyre 1357 for Delamere and Mondrum: NA: 33/6. I am grateful to Mr T. Bland for this reference.
11. Bott, 'Cornmill sites', XI, 57–63.
12. Bott, 'Cornmill sites', XIII, 33.
13. Bott, 'Cornmill sites', XIV, 30.
14. Bott, 'Cornmill sites', XIV, 34.
15. Baker-Wilbraham MSS, 21 April 1692: CALS: DBW/L/F, item 4.
16. Indenture 12 November 1692: Private Ownership of Dr A.J.P. Campbell (collection originally owned by Canon Ridgway), hereafter Campbell Collection. The author is indebted to Dr Campbell for the loan of documents from his collection.
17. 'Fulling mills of the Isle of Wight'.
18. Indenture 30 November 1703: Campbell Collection.
19. Indenture 25 March 1721: Campbell Collection.
20. Receipt/settlement 15 February 1727: Campbell Collection.
21. Tripartite indenture 20 December 1727: Campbell Collection.
22. Letters of Administration, will and codicil of John Beard: CALS: WC 1725–26; WS 1725.
23. CALS: Will of John Waine, 1728 (WS 1728).
24. Baker-Wilbraham MSS, 1802: CALS: DBW/G, packet B, item 5.
25. CALS: Will of Richard Howell, 1815; see also CALS: DBW/G, item 3, dated 1787.
26. I am indebted to Mr M. Kennerley for this information taken from the Primitive Methodists Chester Circuit, 1825.
27. P.P. Burdett, *Survey of the County Palatine of Chester* (1777), with an introduction by J.B. Harley and P. Laxton (Hist. Soc. Lancs. Ches., Occasional series, 1, 1974), 25–26; Bryant,

Map (1831). See also A.D.M. Phillips and C.B. Phillips, *A New Historical Atlas of Cheshire* (Chester, 2002), 67.

28. Tithe map and apportionment for Foulk Stapleford, Tarvin, 1838: CALS: EDT 160/1–2.
29. J.H. Norris, 'The water-powered corn mills of Cheshire', *TLCAS*, LXXV–LXXVI (1965–66), 33–71. Offprint available from CALS: D4744/20 (1969).
30. S.R. Williams, *West Cheshire from the Air* (Chester, 1997), 61.
31. B. Poole, 'Archaeological Monitoring Report for land at Walk Mill, Chester' (unpubl., June 2008).

Colour Plates

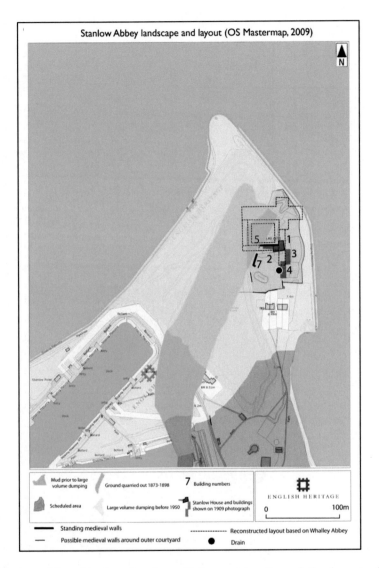

Plate 1. Map showing the theoretical reconstruction of the layout of Stanlow Abbey, the subject of Paper 1, in relation to Stanlow House and the major phases of landscape change on Stanlow Point.

Plate 2. Stanlow Abbey. Medieval walling which may be the southern part of the monastic cloister and building on its south side, possibly the refectory. These walls were probably later incorporated into structures within the monastic grange and post-Dissolution farm buildings (Buildings 2 and 5) considered in Paper 1. At the far end, hidden by the vegetation, is the doorway illustrated in Figure 4 of that paper.

Colour Plates

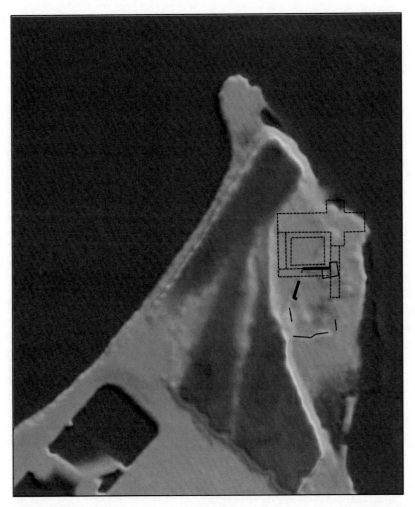

Plate 3. Lidar digital terrain model of Stanlow Point, discussed in Paper 1. The colour bands show red tones for the highest ground (top of the modern waste mounds), grading down through yellow, green, light blue and for the lowest ground (6 m and below) dark blue. This model shows that the outer courtyard would be prone to flooding during tidal or storm surges.

Plate 4. Aerial view, 1983, of the curvilinear enclosure at Hadlow, Willaston, analysed in Paper 2. Almost all the arc of the enclosure can still be traced.

Colour Plates

Plate 5. Trefor Uchaf D/SJ2442: a narrowly dispersed industrial settlement, as defined in Paper 3. Eighteenth- and nineteenth-century industrial remains associated with the lime industry and a dispersed linear settlement, originally of quarrymen's cottages, lie within a rural landscape of dispersed farms and irregular fields of medieval and late medieval origin.

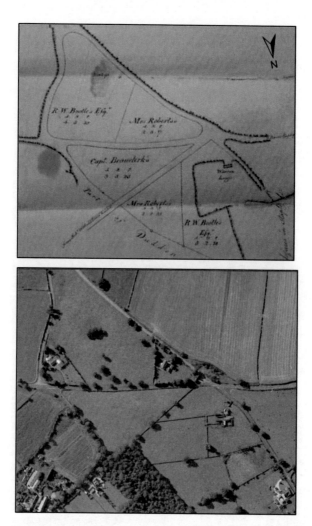

Plate 6. Enclosure map, 1780, and modern field pattern: the common at Burton near Tarvin, considered in Paper 4. The enclosure of this small common was achieved through a signed memorandum of agreement between the proprietors. It continues to govern the pattern of fields and lanes, as indicated by the aerial photograph of the early 1990s.

Colour Plates

Plate 7. Aerial view of Clotton, 2010, referred to in Paper 4, showing contrasting patterns of enclosure to north and south of the settlement. This aerial view depicts field patterns indicative of different enclosure processes. Compare the narrow reverse-S fields of the former open arable area to the south with the straight hedges produced by formal enclosure of the common to the north.

Plate 8. The recently reconstructed Walk Mill, Foulk Stapleford, on the River Gowy, the subject of Paper 5, showing the feed to the Mill Wheel: now in operation as a corn grinding mill.

Plate 9. Sunnyside, Baschurch, illustrative of Paper 6: an early seventeenth-century, L shaped timber-framed building. Brick infilling between the timbers was a feature of seventeenth-century houses in Baschurch: a visual sign in the landscape of the wealth and status of the owners.

Plate 10. The crossroads in the centre of Disley village, referred to in Paper 7, looking north west. The road straight ahead is the original Buxton-Manchester turnpike of 1725, which from here climbs steeply up the slope of Jackson's Edge. At the foot of the hill it is crossed at right angles by the replacement turnpike of the early 1820s, now the sinuously curving and easily graded A6.

Colour Plates

Plate 11. The old and new Buxton turnpikes east of Macclesfield, discussed in Paper 7, looking east from a point just above Greenways Farm. The old road (turnpiked in 1759) is on the right and is just wide enough for two vehicles to pass. It can also be seen in the distance, approaching the narrow valley of Stake Clough. The completely new turnpike built from 1821 to 1827 is to the left: although broader and far better graded, it is significantly longer. Its route is marked by the gentle diagonal line climbing the slope of Shining Tor in the middle distance. Both roads are aiming for the *Cat and Fiddle*, prominent on the skyline.

165

Plate 12. Clayton's Tower, Windmill Lane, on the Bollington side of Kerridge hill. This stone turret, referred to in Paper 8, bears quarry and coal master William Clayton's initials on its western side. It is believed to be an ornamental chimney shaft built in the early 1840s for a steam engine associated with a coal mine. A flue running downhill from the chimney shows no evidence of having been used and the near-contemporary building at the lower end of the flue does not have the distinctive features of a former engine house. Plans to expand mining operations to the west side of Kerridge hill died with Clayton in 1851 but the tower stands today as a memorial to his ambitions.

6

BLACK AND WHITE HOUSES
TO BLACK AND WHITE COWS:
THE FARMING ECONOMY OF A SHROPSHIRE PARISH

Sharon M. Varey

Introduction

Shropshire as a county, and the northern plain in particular, is often overlooked in landscape history studies. For this reason, the writer decided to take a closer look at the landscape of a small area of north west Shropshire with this paper focusing upon the farming economy of the ancient parish of Baschurch *c.*1550 to 2000 (Figures 1 and 2). Located on the north Shropshire plain, this large multi-township parish, covering in excess of 8,000 acres, lies approximately seven miles north west of Shrewsbury; an area large enough to reveal significant trends, yet small enough to facilitate detailed research.

With the exception of Edwards's research on the northern plain and Hey's work on the neighbouring parish of Myddle, carried out over thirty years ago and focusing upon the period *c.*1550 to 1700, little detailed historical research has been carried out in this part of Shropshire. The writer wished to discover to what extent trends discerned elsewhere on the northern plain and in Shropshire as a whole were applicable to the study area, whether these trends continued throughout the period and the extent to which these trends were reflected in the landscape.[1]

For the purposes of this paper, analysis of the period *c.*1550 to 1750 draws upon an extensive collection of surviving probate inventories, whereas evidence for the later period, post-1750, consists of estate surveys, tithe data, board of trade figures, sale

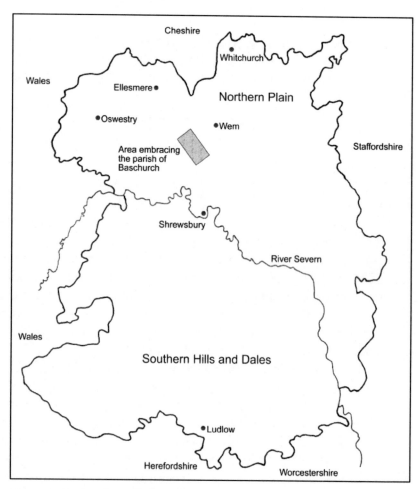

Figure 1. The location of Baschurch.

particulars and oral sources. This inevitably means that the approaches pre- and post-1750 are different: the first considers the proportion of crops and livestock in terms of the overall wealth of the individual with the inventories giving a very detailed impression of how the land was used upon individual

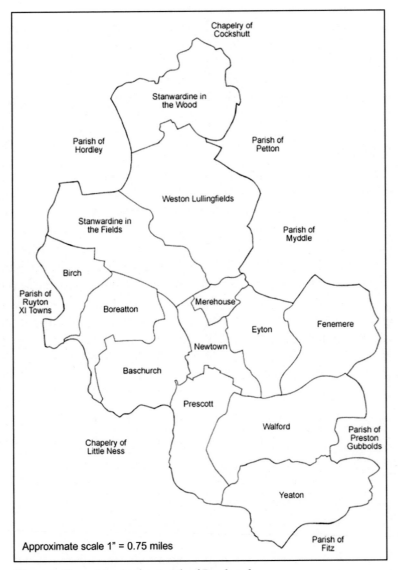

Figure 2. Townships in the parish of Baschurch.

farms throughout the townships on a decadal basis, whereas the second considers the changes that have taken place in terms of the acreage devoted to livestock and crops, giving a snapshot of a township or the parish at various points in time. This diversity of approach needs to be borne in mind when analysing the trends taking place pre- and post-1750.

1550–1750

Analysis of over 300 probate inventories, spread throughout the townships, revealed a number of significant trends. The percentage of inventories mentioning cattle, sheep and horses declined during the period 1550 to 1750, but as Table 1 shows, herd and flock sizes increased, suggesting greater specialisation was occurring in the farming economy. Median herd and flock sizes were larger in Baschurch (Table 2) than Edwards found for the northern plain as a whole. Although Edwards only used selected decades to define trends, the evidence would appear to suggest that both cattle and sheep were a more important part of the rural economy in the study area than on the north Shropshire plain as a whole.

Period	Cattle	Sheep	Horses
1550–1599	11.70	25.42	1.93
1600–1649	12.17	37.74	2.25
1650–1699	12.09	26.80	2.08
1700–1749	16.65	40.44	3.42

Table 1. Average herd and flock sizes, 1550–1749.

An important consideration in the context of cattle herds is the development of dairy farming. Edwards has noted its 'remarkable expansion' in the north east of the county during the seventeenth century.[2] In Baschurch the evidence suggests that this development occurred in two distinctive phases (Table 3). The first phase occurred during the first half of the seventeenth century; amounts of produce were often small, amounting to 10s or less and were most likely intended for domestic consumption. Farmers producing butter and cheese in larger quantities, valued at between £1 and £5, tended to have a dairy herd of seven or more cows alongside sizeable flocks of sheep and beef cattle. Joice Porter, a widow from Yeaton who died in 1614, had a herd of eight milk cows with produce worth five pounds. Similarly, Thomas Williams of Walford had a herd of seven cows and produce amounting to £2 6s 8d when he died in 1615. The inventories reveal that dairy farming on this scale was taking place throughout the parish with the produce being sold at local markets.

The second phase in the development of dairy farming took place during the first half of the eighteenth century. The inventories reveal that dairy herds were often significantly larger than they had been in the first half of the seventeenth century with the evidence suggesting that large amounts of cheese were being produced for commercial sale (Figure 3).

Individuals such as Edward Tomkies, a yeoman of Fenemere who died in 1701, had thirteen milk cows with a stock of cheese and butter worth thirty pounds. As well as the county fairs, it seems likely that this cheese was supplying either the London market via the Cheshire ports or was being transported on the River Severn to outlets in Worcester, Gloucester and Bristol.[3] A significant feature of this second phase was the emergence of 'dairy townships' across the parish. In both Stanwardine in the Wood and Fenemere, farmers had larger dairy herds and were producing considerable amounts of cheese for commercial sale.

Period	Cattle		Sheep		Horses	
	Northern Plain	Baschurch	Northern Plain	Baschurch	Northern Plain	Baschurch
1550s	9–10	14	30	50	2	2
1660s	9	11	17	43	2	2
1740s	18–19	20	10–12	50	4	5

Table 2. Median herd and flock sizes: a comparison with Edwards's data for the northern plain.

Period	% inventories mentioning dairy produce
1550–1599	12.12
1600–1649	45.71
1650–1699	28.95
1700–1749	41.86

Table 3. Percentage of inventories mentioning dairy produce, 1550–1749.

Dairying had been an important feature of the farming economy in Stanwardine in the Wood since the sixteenth century. Perhaps the first serious dairy farmer was Griffith Edwards. Although no produce was listed in his inventory of c.1536, he owned ten milk cows alongside twelve pigs. This was a sizeable herd when average parish dairy herds amounted to four beasts. Edwards's pigs would have been a valuable side-line to his livestock for they could be fed on the dairy waste. A more substantial herd of dairy cows was owned by Thomas Corbet. He had twenty-six milk cows in addition to his other livestock. Although he only had dairy produce worth three

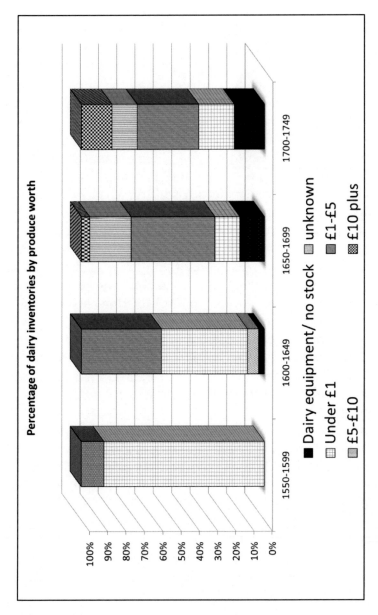

Figure 3. Value of dairy produce, 1550–1749.

pounds in November 1615, his twenty-four pigs additionally testify to his dairying enterprise. Dairying continued to prosper in this township. In 1662 Roger Acherley had twelve milk cows and produce amounting to fourteen pounds and in 1711, Robert Joy had nineteen dairy cows, swine, plus other livestock with dairy produce amounting to thirty pounds.

Why did specialisation occur in specific areas of the parish? The 'key' would appear to be landholding. Both the townships of Stanwardine in the Wood and Fenemere were in dual ownership by the early eighteenth century, which facilitated the creation of larger consolidated farms – a necessary prerequisite to accommodating larger dairy herds. It would seem likely that this situation had prevailed in Stanwardine in the Wood since the sixteenth century. Additionally the heavy clay soil of the township suited dairying. This situation was in contrast to other parts of the parish where multiple landownership existed, often resulting in smaller farms and fragmented holdings.[4] Larger commercial enterprises were able to operate economies of scale and take advantage of the improved marketing outlets for cheese. The evidence thus suggests a direct link between the type of landholding, dairy herd size and the scale of cheese production.

Sheep rearing was an important part of the farming economy in north-west Shropshire. Specialisation was taking place as overall flock sizes increased despite a decline in the percentage of inventories mentioning sheep from 80.30% in the period 1550 to 1599 to 55.81% in the period 1700 to 1749. The percentage of inventories mentioning wool experienced a similar decline from 21.42% in the period 1600 to 1649 to just 10.47% 100 years later. The largest flocks in the parish (often in excess of 100 animals) were to be found in the southern townships of Yeaton, Newtown, Baschurch and Little Ness, from which there was easy access by road to wool markets in both Oswestry and Shrewsbury. Field names too suggest the importance of sheep rearing with 'Yesters' referring to an area of sheepfolds in the township of Newtown.[5] It is interesting to note that Richard Gough, writing primarily about the neighbouring parish of Myddle in 1701, refers to 'the wool of Baschurch and Nesse which bears the name of the best in this county',[6] suggesting that this small area of the county was renowned for its produce.

Crops were a subsidiary element of the local economy. Although a variety of crops were grown, the percentage of inventories mentioning cereals declined during the early modern period.[7] Nevertheless, comparison with data from the Telford and Severn Gorge parishes reveals that cereal crops were a more important component of the rural economy of Baschurch than of parishes further south in the county.[8] Barley was particularly suited to the lighter soils of the south of the parish. Numerous references to 'heareclothes', 'mault' mills, 'weeting vessells' and malt chambers amongst the inventories suggest that a considerable proportion of the crop was used in malting and brewing in addition to its use as a cereal and as animal feed. New crops, including grasses, were introduced during the mid-seventeenth century and by the 1690s, clover was being grown on the farms of Richard Palin (1693) and William Tydder (1694). However, the number of inventories mentioning clover remained small, even in the eighteenth century, and was localised in its extent, being favoured on the lighter soils of the southern townships.

Further analysis of the inventories revealed that the proportion of a farmer's 'wealth' devoted to the farming enterprise declined during the period 1550 to 1750 in favour of possessions and other assets. Table 4 shows how the percentage devoted to livestock, crops and produce (LCP) declined from 67.78% during the second half of the sixteenth century to just

45.23% by the first half of the eighteenth century with a corresponding increase in the percentage devoted to possessions and other assets. This suggests the average farmer was becoming sufficiently prosperous that he could spend a greater proportion of his livelihood on household items, clothes and money lending.

Period	% Devoted to livestock, crops and produce	% Possessions	% Other
1550–1599	67.78	20.86	11.36
1600–1649	52.14	25.25	22.61
1650–1699	47.30	24.51	28.19
1700–1749	45.23	29.32	25.45

Table 4. Breakdown of inventory 'wealth' through time.

Evidence of the prosperity of early modern farming can be found in the landscape of the parish, for there are a number of timber framed dwellings dating from the second half of the sixteenth century and early seventeenth century (Figures 4 and 5). In Yeaton, 12.50% of the inventories for the period 1550 to 1599 are valued at over £100, a figure which increased to 41.67% in the period 1600 to 1649 and 50% in the following fifty year period, 1650 to 1699. This prosperity is borne out further for the inventories reveal a decline in the proportion of 'wealth' directly devoted to the farming enterprise from 67.94% in the period 1550 to 1599 to just 33.12% between 1600 to 1649 suggesting there was spare capital for spending on houses and their furnishings. Although this figure increased to 45.44% during the period 1650 to 1699 it still suggests a relatively prosperous farming community who were able to invest a

Figure 4. Bailiff's House, Yeaton (rear view). Mid- to late sixteenth century, L-shaped with a hall and cross wing. An additional storey was added in the nineteenth century.

substantial percentage of their profits enhancing their domestic life by improving their living conditions.[9]

Building activity based upon farming prosperity can be seen elsewhere in the parish. In the dairying township of Stanwardine in the Wood, Stanwardine Hall, an original timber framed structure, was embedded in brick and substantially remodelled during the latter part of the sixteenth and early seventeenth centuries. At Wycherley Hall, a storeyed porch was added to the timber framed structure in the late sixteenth century and a long hall range was added in the early years of the seventeenth century. This was followed by a new porch and then by a cross wing with further gables to the front and rear in the later seventeenth century. The bold decorative framing of Wycherley Hall and the use of brick and stone at Stanwardine Hall ensured that these substantial houses proclaimed the wealth and status of the owners and their farming enterprises for all to see.

Figure 5. Plumtree Cottage, Yeaton. Mid- to late seventeenth century with later nineteenth-century additions.

In the centre of Baschurch village, there are a number of timber framed houses which were either constructed during the seventeenth century or remodelled then (Figure 6 and Plate 9). Previously such a trend might have been interpreted as part of Hoskins's 'great rebuilding'.[10] However, this concept has been modified, renamed and even abandoned by scholars in more recent years.[11] Moran has noted that the brick infilling on these seventeenth century timber framed dwellings was integral at the outset[12] – a feature which could be interpreted as an additional visual sign of wealth and status.

It would indeed seem reasonable to suggest that this flurry of building activity, visible in various parts of the parish, was

Figure 6. The Hollies, Baschurch. T shaped with a fifteenth-century cruck framed hall range. Remodelled in the early seventeenth century with a two bay framed cross wing.

the result of agricultural prosperity, brought about by the rise of dairy farming, supported by the profits from wool. The evidence from Baschurch is in contrast to the rest of the county for Mercer has commented upon a lack of building activity dating from the late sixteenth and seventeenth centuries in Shropshire generally – a fact which points to the distinctive character of this northern parish.[13]

1750–2000

To what extent did these trends in pastoral farming continue after 1750? Estate surveys from the 1770s would indicate a trend towards arable farming. They reveal that a greater proportion of the land on farms on both the Walford and Boreatton estates was given over to arable production – a trend which would appear to have increased by the 1840s when the Tithe survey was carried out.[14] It is interesting to note that Hey came to the same conclusion as a result of his research in neighbouring Myddle, for he states that there was a 'profound change' in the farming economy from pastoral to arable farming during the late eighteenth and early part of the nineteenth century.[15] In considering why this should be the case, consideration must be given to the situation nationally. The writer would suggest that the increase in arable lands was a reflection of and a response to the growing population of the eighteenth and nineteenth centuries, and in particular a response to the growing urban populations of Manchester, Liverpool and the West Midlands. This situation was exacerbated by war. Conflict with France (1793–1815) led to an increase in cereal production in Shropshire generally.[16]

Estate records and maps record these changes in the landscape of the parish. Landowners such as the Hunts of Boreatton were reorganising their fields and farms in order to farm more productively. Similarly, R.A. Slaney, upon inheriting land in Prescott, purchased additional fields and exchanged existing farmlands with neighbouring landowners to create a consolidated holding. Thereafter, field boundaries were straightened and fields amalgamated in order to make the land more productive and create a consolidated estate.[17]

Tithe data suggests that the proportion of land given over to arable farming was lowest in the northern townships of Stanwardine in the Wood and Weston Lullingfields indicating that pastoral farming was still of considerable importance in this part of the parish. Additionally, the tithe files for a number of the southern townships including Fenemere and Eyton suggest that there were still sizeable flocks and dairy herds kept on the farms of these townships although the acreage devoted to arable was in the ascendancy. It is important to remember that by the fourth decade of the nineteenth century, improvements in grazing land meant that a larger number of animals could be kept on smaller amounts of pasture. Taken together, one could conclude that there was an increase in the proportion of arable land but that the apparent contrast in the rural economy before and after 1750 might not have been as stark as first appeared and could in part be due to the nature of the available evidence.

From the middle of the nineteenth century the evidence suggests that livestock were once again at the forefront of the Baschurch economy. Figure 7 shows the upward trend in cow numbers from the mid-nineteenth century whilst figure 8 reveals the slump in wheat acreages after 1870.[18] This trend reflects the situation nationally for cheap foreign imports were affecting the growth and trade in cereals resulting in a period of 'agricultural depression' for cereal growers. However, livestock farmers were in a better position to weather the storm.

Notwithstanding the situation nationally, the 'key' to the economic fortunes of Baschurch during the later nineteenth century and early decades of the twentieth century, was the railway station. Located about half a mile from the existing settlement of Newtown, on a 'greenfield' site, the railway became important for the transportation of livestock and liquid milk. A fortnightly auction was set up alongside the station which attracted butchers and buyers from as far afield as Birmingham, Wolverhampton and Dudley in the West Midlands. However, the 'bright spot' in English agriculture in the later nineteenth century was the liquid milk trade.[19] Milk was sent from local parishes via the station at Baschurch to

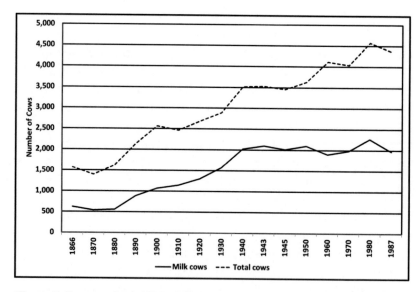

Figure 7. Cow numbers, 1866–1987.

Manchester, Birmingham, Liverpool and London. Locally, the trade developed alongside cheese production and by 1921 a dairy had been set up in the village. It distributed milk alongside producing butter and cheese.

Cheese continued to be made on the farms during the 1920s and 1930s and was sold at the large cheese fairs held in Wem, Shrewsbury and Ellesmere. At Nill Green farm, in Stanwardine in the Wood, 60 lb cheeses were made from February to October for sale at the Manchester Co-op. Sale particulars dating to 1920 reveal the farm had a milk room, press house and cheese room, in addition to a dairy and whey house. As the shippon could accommodate 80 cows, these particulars give some indication of the extent of the dairy concern. A similar picture is conveyed by the farm at Stanwardine Hall which in 1920 was able to accommodate 94 cows in addition to its dairy, press house and cheese room.

182

Dairies and cheese rooms were also a common feature of the larger farms in Fenemere although herd sizes were smaller ranging between 26 and 50 animals.[20]

The importance of dairy farming in this area continued throughout the twentieth century, although by the end of the Second World War the production of cheese in Shropshire was 'almost non-existent.'[21] Mechanised milking parlours became a feature of local farms and, combined with the introduction of the Friesian herd, led to substantial increases in liquid milk production. By 1971 there were 21 specialist dairy farms in the parish. This figure has declined latterly mirroring the situation nationally.[22] Today the majority of the dairy farms are located towards the north of the parish.

Although dairy farming has and continues to be an important element of the farming economy, it is important to remember that other types of livestock have continued to play an important role. Sheep, pigs and beef cattle have long been an important element of the economy. However, during the second half of the twentieth century increasing specialisation in the rearing of livestock has taken place which has resulted in separate dairy, beef or pig farms rather than a mixed farming enterprise. Once, an important sideline to the dairy farmer, the keeping of pigs has become a separate farming enterprise with intensive indoor production. The keeping of poultry has been similarly transformed with the factory farming of hens from the 1950s and more recently the rise in demand for free-range eggs. Although specialist livestock farming is in evidence on many farms of the parish, a considerable proportion of the land is often given over to arable crops, most commonly wheat, barley, sugar beet, beans and peas.

Figure 8 reveals the trends in wheat, barley and sugar beet production during the twentieth century. The graph shows the

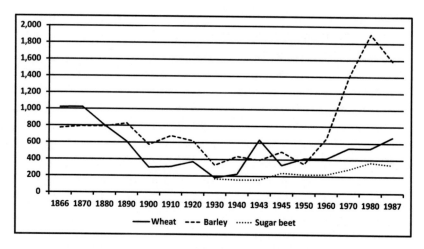

Figure 8. Wheat, barley and sugar beet acreages, 1866–1987.

dramatic increase in wheat acreages during the Second World War, a trend which was reflected in neighbouring parishes, as the government offered cash incentives to farmers who ploughed up their permanent grassland. Since 1960 wheat acreages have increased on a modest scale throughout the parish. Although the acreage fluctuated, barley continued to be a popular crop during the second half of the nineteenth century and into the twentieth century as it was well suited to Shropshire soils. Since the 1960s barley has experienced a boom in acreage. The cultivation of sugar beet became popular in many Shropshire parishes during the 1920s and by 1930 a considerable acreage in Baschurch was devoted to the crop – its popularity stemming from the fact the tops and dried pulp could be used as animal fodder.

During the nineteenth century turnips were an important vegetable crop with many farms possessing separate turnip houses.[23] Acreages declined after 1870 but turnips were still an important part of the farming economy until the arrival of

184

sugar beet. The growth of peas was popularised by Colonel Eyton of Walford who set up a canning factory on his estate in the early 1930s. Such was the success of the venture that he employed 200 people on a seasonal basis canning peas and other local produce.[24] By the 1950s, 'Baschurch Quick Frozen Foods' was set up in the old dairy. This concern processed peas along with other fruits and vegetables until the 1960s.[25] Peas and beans continue to be grown in the parish today although the former are now used as animal feed.

Later twentieth-century farming methods involving greater specialisation and larger herd sizes have had an impact on the landscape of certain parts of the parish. A number of field boundaries have altered as fields have been amalgamated to aid the production of arable farming. In both the townships of Baschurch and Stanwardine in the Wood nineteenth-century brick built farm buildings have been demolished or converted into housing. Nineteenth-century accommodation for livestock is in many instances no longer 'fit for purpose.' This has led to the construction of 'industrial estate' style buildings to accommodate livestock. In one instance this has additionally involved the relocation of both the farmhouse and its buildings, with the construction of a modern farmhouse and new livestock accommodation, accessed via the main road approaching the village. The old farmhouse (sited close to the church in the centre of the village) has subsequently been renovated and the nineteenth-century livestock accommodation has been converted into housing.

Summary

The farming economy of Baschurch was predominantly pastoral throughout the early modern period. This paper has shown that specialisation was taking place. There was an increase in herd and flock sizes by the first half of the eighteenth century despite the percentage of people keeping livestock decreasing. An in-depth analysis of probate inventories has shown that the largest flocks of sheep were located in the southern townships of the parish. It has also revealed that the rise of dairy farming within the parish occurred in two phases. The first phase was on a small scale, herd sizes were small and produce was intended primarily for local or domestic consumption. This phase occurred throughout the parish. The second phase was characterised by large herds kept on substantial farms. Evidence would suggest that there was a direct link between the type of landholding, dairy herd size and the scale of cheese production. To what extent this pattern can be discerned in other North Shropshire parishes would be worthy of future research.

The inventories additionally revealed that during the period 1550 to 1750 there was a decline in 'wealth' devoted to the farming enterprise, suggesting that the average farmer was becoming more prosperous, investing more capital in furnishings and possessions than hitherto. The landscape of the parish contains numerous examples of the wealth of the livestock farmers during the seventeenth century when they were building anew or remodelling their existing homes.

Although livestock has been the mainstay of the Baschurch economy since the sixteenth century, the balance between livestock and crops has fluctuated, often in response to the situation nationally as in times of population growth and conflict overseas when cereal production increased substantially. Despite changes in the proportion of pasture to arable fields, a strong element of continuity pervaded the rural economy of the parish throughout the period. Change occurred, especially during the twentieth century, as farms switched direction and new specialist enterprises emerged. However, a mixed approach to farming continues to pervade the parish in the opening decades of the twenty-first century.[26]

References

1. P.R. Edwards, 'The Farming Economy of North East Shropshire in the Seventeenth Century' (University of Oxford PhD thesis, 1976); P.R. Edwards, 'The development of dairy farming on the north Shropshire plain in the seventeenth century', *Midland History*, IV (1978), 175–90; D.G. Hey, *An English Rural Community: Myddle Under the Tudors and Stuarts* (Leicester, 1974). See also J.P. Dodd, 'Shropshire Agriculture 1793–1870' (University of London PhD thesis, 1981); *VCH Shrops*, IV; S.M. Varey, 'Society and the Land – the Changing Landscape of Baschurch, North Shropshire *c*.1550–2000' (University of Liverpool PhD thesis, 2009).
2. Edwards, 'Development of dairy farming', 177.
3. C. Foster, 'Cheshire cheese: farming in the North West in the seventeenth and eighteenth centuries', *THSLC*, CXLIV (1995), 26.
4. Varey, 'Society and the Land', 65–155.
5. Five adjoining fields have this name on the Boreatton estate survey, 1775: SA: 6000/16971, but the name probably dates back to the sixteenth century. Grant of the Manor of Baschurch: SA: 6000/17285.
6. R. Gough, *The History of Myddle*, ed. D. Hey (Harmondsworth, 1981), 265. 'Nesse' = Little Ness.
7. Varey, 'Society and the Land', 185, table 4.25.
8. Varey, 'Society and the Land', 187, table 4.26.
9. This picture is in contrast to the situation in Yeaton by the first half of the eighteenth century. 70% of the inventories

for the period 1700 to 1749 are valued at less than £20 and there are no inventories valued in excess of £100 – a situation which is similarly reflected in the landscape, for there is a distinct lack of eighteenth-century building.

10. W.G. Hoskins, 'The rebuilding of rural England 1570–1640' in W.G. Hoskins, ed., *Provincial England: Essays in Social and Economic History* (London, 1964), 131–48.

11. J. Groves, 'Houses in north-east Cheshire in the age of the Great Rebuilding, 1600–1760', *Ches.Hist.*, XXV (1990), 30–39; D. Hey, 'Introduction' in P.S. Barnwell and M. Airs, eds., *Houses and the Hearth Tax: The Later Stuart House and Society* (York, 2006).

12. M. Moran, *Vernacular Buildings of Shropshire* (Almeley, 2003), 91.

13. E. Mercer, *English Architecture to 1900: The Shropshire Experience* (Almeley, 2003), 151.

14. Varey, 'Society and the Land', 201–4.

15. Hey, *An English Rural Community*, 68.

16. *VCH Shrops*, IV, 181.

17. Varey, 'Society and the Land', 69–81 and 88–90.

18. Board of Trade Agricultural Returns: TNA: MAFF68 nos. 57–58, 257, 713, 1283, 1853, 2423, 2987, 3527, 3954, 4065, 4139, 4324, 4694, 5190, 5716, 6074.

19. J.R. Walton, 'Agriculture and rural society 1730–1914' in R.A. Dodgson and R.A. Butlin, eds., *An Historical Geography of England and Wales* (2nd edn, London, 1990), 343.

20. Petton Park Estate Sale Particulars, 1920: SA: Sc/2/77; Fenemere Estate Sale Particulars, 1911, courtesy of Mr R. Gough, Fenemere Manor.

21. N. Bennett, *Survey Report for the Development Plan for Shropshire* (Shrewsbury, 1952), 16.

22. TNA: MAFF68/5190 and MAFF6074. M.H.R. Soper and E.S. Carter, *Modern Farming and the Countryside: The Issues in Perspective* (London, 1985), 22.
23. SA: Sc/2/77; Fenemere Estate Sale Particulars, 1911, courtesy of Mr R. Gough, Fenemere Manor.
24. E.C. Wadlow, 'A Description and History of Walford' (unpubl., 1985), E10.09; I. Williams, *Baschurch Memoirs*, compiled by O. Peppiatt (Shrewsbury, 1997), 58.
25. C. Mytton-Davies, *Baschurch Memoirs*, 2; Mrs M. Topham, oral communication, 18/02/02.
26. A more in-depth analysis of the farming economy can be found in Varey, 'Society and the Land', 157–228.

7

NEW ROADS FOR OLD:
CHESHIRE TURNPIKES IN THE LANDSCAPE, 1700–1850

Alan G. Crosby

In its heyday, in the mid-nineteenth century, the network of turnpike roads in Cheshire covered approximately 590 miles, providing an interconnected and well-developed system of major highways.[1] It had emerged piecemeal over a period of 120 years from the mid-1720s, the last piece of this complicated jigsaw being put in place in the mid-1850s when for twenty years the roads had been facing the challenge of the growing railway network. The landscape impact of turnpike roads is considerable. In parts of the historic county, especially north of Macclesfield and east of Warrington, and in the northern part of Wirral, they were key determinants of the developing geography of the conurbations, helping to shape industrial and residential growth. Most of the county's main road network, from the long descent from the *Cat and Fiddle* towards Macclesfield in the east, via the broad alignments of the A50 in mid-Cheshire, to the intricate pattern of local routes between Hoylake and Birkenhead, was shaped and in many cases built from scratch by turnpike trusts, laying the foundations for the motor age which began a couple of decades after the demise of the trusts themselves.

This paper considers the growth of the turnpike network from these perspectives, focusing on the rationale behind road development, the geographical pattern of the network, and its physical characteristics. Matters such as administration, management and finance are not dealt with here, though it is essential to recognise that these factors were also important in shaping the emerging network.[2] Throughout, the paper takes as its geographical area the historic county of Cheshire, as it existed before the 1930s.

Background

The idea of the turnpike road was a response to the inadequacies of the existing system of highway administration, which had been established by an Act of 1555. That placed responsibility for road maintenance squarely upon the parish (or, in the northern counties, the township), which was perhaps realistic in the reign of Mary I but by that of George I was manifestly inadequate to deal with the growing volume of traffic on inter-urban or inter-regional routes, and with the demands posed by economic and demographic expansion. The fragmentation of administration produced extremely variable standards of upkeep, was wastefully incoherent, and imposed serious financial burdens upon the communities through which roads passed. The problem was clear: between Chester and Nantwich, for example, the present A51 traversed seventeen separate townships, each responsible for its own short stretch of road (Figure 1). The highways were the subject of constant complaint. Grumbling about the roads has been an English national pastime for half a millennium so we should not take the grievances at face value, but there is no doubt that the expanding economy, growing population and increased traffic did present considerable challenges. Evidence from south-east Lancashire shows that the growth of Manchester produced major problems as heavy goods traffic heading for the town damaged road surfaces and made the upkeep of bridges ever more troublesome.[3]

By 1663 the condition of the Great North Road in Hertfordshire and Huntingdonshire had deteriorated to such an extent that the county justices secured powers, by

Figure 1. The old London-Chester highway at Hockenhull Platts, south of Tarvin, where the road crosses the present and former channels of the River Gowy on three linked packhorse bridges. The narrow and winding road, which eastwards from the river is no wider than a footpath, was briefly part of the Nantwich and Chester turnpike (1744) before being superseded by the present A51 to the north (1759).

parliamentary Act, to take over a stretch of the road (and thus remove responsibility from the parishes en route) and fund improved maintenance by charging tolls. This, the first turnpike Act, was not met with enthusiasm – the next Acts were not passed until 1695, and by 1702 there had been only six. Administration by justices was soon replaced by the principle of independent bodies of trustees, likewise deriving their powers from parliament, who managed specified stretches of road and could not only charge tolls but also raise money by fixed interest bonds. Their powers were normally granted for a specified period, at the end of which they would either lapse or be renewed by further legislation.

The seventh Act, passed in 1705, was for the Hatton-Barnhill section of the road from Chester to Whitchurch and the midlands. This first Cheshire example thus came early in the history of turnpikes, but it was a very limited project, covering only five miles and distantly isolated from any other improvement. The preamble to the Act stated that the road was in decay, partly because of the 'great and many loads and heavy carriages of cheese and other goods' which used the route, but it is not clear why this section was specifically chosen. The area was low-lying and crossed by small streams, and drainage was certainly a problem, but it is not impossible that the influence of the bishop of Chester, whose summer residence at Broxton was close to the southern end of the turnpiked section, may have been a factor. It remained the only turnpike in northern England for another twenty years, apart from the 1714 project to improve the north-south road through Staffordshire, from Tittensor near Stone, through Newcastle-under-Lyme, to the Cheshire border near Church Lawton.

The great inter-regional roads
By the 1720s turnpiking of inter-urban roads in southern England and the south midlands was well-advanced, stimulating support for improvements to the arterial routes of the north midlands. In 1725 an Act was passed for the road from Hurdlow south of Buxton, through Buxton town and Chapel-en-le-Frith, to Whaley Bridge, Disley, Stockport and Manchester, part of the great high road from London via Manchester to Carlisle. It was one of the most important national routes, but the special significance was Manchester itself – as one of the fastest-growing towns in the kingdom, with a dynamic commercial sector and a powerful role as a regional market centre, the town became the focus of numerous turnpike projects. In 1728 the existing turnpike from Stone to the Cheshire border was reconstituted and extended

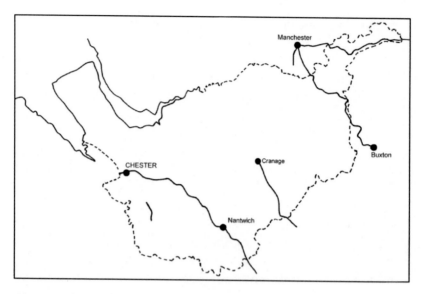

Figure 2. Cheshire roads turnpiked before 1750.

southwards to Lichfield. Two years later it was extended further under a new Act by the turnpiking of the road through Arclid and Holmes Chapel to Cranage Green. In 1731 an Act was passed for the road from Manchester to Ashton-under-Lyne and Staley Bridge,[4] and then via Mottram in Longdendale to Woodhead and the Yorkshire border, high on the watershed at Saltersbrook. The Yorkshire continuation remained unimproved until an Act of 1741 authorised turnpiking between Saltersbrook and Doncaster via Penistone with a branch to Rotherham. In 1743 another existing turnpike, from Coleshill in Warwickshire through Staffordshire, was extended from Woore via Nantwich, Tarporley and Tarvin to Chester, along the line of the present A51 (Figure 2).

In each case, for Cheshire roads as for those in any other part of the country, a relatively standardised preamble stated the rationale for the proposal:

the highway was by reason of the nature of the soil, and of the many and heavy Carriages frequently passing through the same ... become so ruinous and bad, that in Winter season many parts thereof are impassable for Waggons and Carriages, and very dangerous for Travellers, and cannot by the ordinary course appointed by the Laws and Statutes of the Realm be effectually mended.[5]

Such wording is so characteristic that it cannot necessarily be regarded as an explicit description of the situation. Only occasionally is special reference made to a distinctive local feature: for example, the Doncaster-Saltersbrook turnpike Act of 1741 stated that the road would be 'very convenient for conveying of Goods from the Eastern to the Western Seas' and that the Manchester-Saltersbrook section was already turnpiked and 'very well repaired'.[6]

That quotation emphasises a distinctive feature of these earliest Cheshire turnpikes. It is frequently observed that the turnpike network of England and Wales, like those first of the canals and later of the railways, developed piecemeal and without an overall plan, leading to illogical gaps and wasteful duplication. This is to some extent true. Most were developed without state involvement, and there was never a master plan for a national network. Gaps existed, many roads did not continue to their obvious destination, and the underlying economic rationale was often flawed. But the Cheshire examples demonstrate that even in the 1720s and 1730s some promoters knew that their stretches of road were integral parts of an emergent national and regional network, and that long-distance traffic was an essential element in their use. All the pre-1750 turnpikes in the county formed part of inter-regional routes, from Chester or Manchester to the midlands and London or from 'the Eastern to the Western Seas'.

This focus upon longer-distance routes continued during the 1750s and 1760s, and some projects were notably ambitious: the turnpiking of the road from Chester to Whitchurch, authorised in 1759, was part of a scheme extending via Newport, Wolverhampton and Castle Bromwich to Hampton in Arden, with a branch to Birmingham.[7] The length was such that from the outset the road was managed in four autonomous sections with separate bodies of trustees, but the vision was of a trunk road from London through the West Midlands to Chester and thence by sea to Dublin. Looking only at the network within the county boundary therefore gives a misleading impression. The turnpike from, for example, Alsager to Holmes Chapel certainly had significance for local traffic, but its real importance was as part of a national road from London to Lancashire and beyond. But by the 1750s some promoters also envisaged more complex networks, with branches added to main routes. Thus, the 1756 turnpiking of the road from Wrexham to Chester extended the Shrewsbury-Wrexham scheme of 1752, continuing the 'trunk road' to what was still perceived as the regional capital, but the Act also authorised the turnpiking of link roads to Wem, Ruabon, Ellesmere, Overton and Hanmer, from Saltney to Flint and Holywell, and from Broughton to Mold, creating a sub-regional network spanning four counties.

The chronology and mileage of Cheshire turnpikes
Figure 3 shows the number of Cheshire turnpike Acts grouped by decade from 1700 to 1859, excluding those which only involved the renewal of existing powers but including every Act which authorised new turnpiking of a stretch of road.[8] It

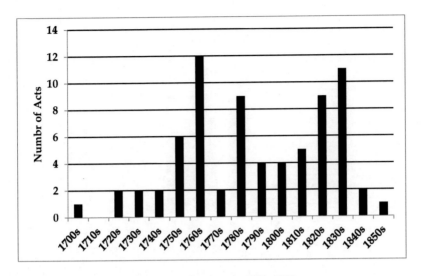

Figure 3. Cheshire turnpike Acts by decade 1700–1859.

demonstrates the relatively slow take-up in the early decades, followed by a dramatic increase in activity in the 1760s. This roughly coincides with the so-called 'turnpike mania' identified from national studies, although the peak in Cheshire was a little earlier than in the country as a whole and rather later than in neighbouring Lancashire.[9] The peak was followed by a sharp fall, as was also the case with the canal and railway manias, although unlike those the turnpike mania did not produce a plethora of wildly over-ambitious or geographically crazy schemes. The lessening of interest in the 1770s was partly because most of the 'obvious' county roads had by then been turnpiked, and partly because the financial capacity of promoters was stretched, not least because canal schemes represented an attractive, if more precarious, alternative opportunity for investment.

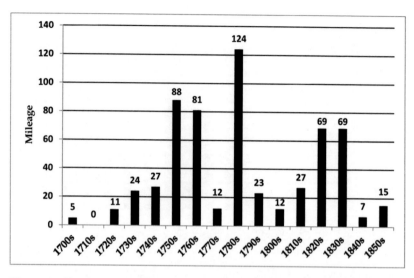

Figure 4. Cheshire turnpikes: mileage authorised by decade 1700–1859.

After 1770 there were no Cheshire turnpike Acts for ten years, but the 1780s saw new enthusiasm, involving roads which differed markedly from the inter-regional routes of the earlier decades. The Industrial Revolution stimulated new traffic flows to be carried and new or enlarged communities to be served, especially in north-east and east Cheshire. Activity lessened during the Napoleonic Wars, from 1795 onwards, but grew rapidly in the 1820s and 1830s. Taking twenty-year periods, and using the number of Acts for new turnpike roads as the criterion, the most important phase of turnpiking in Cheshire was 1820–1840. The development of a modern transport infrastructure was not a sequential process in which one mode succeeded and eclipsed another (turnpikes > canals > railways > roads) but rather a complementary process in which each mode overlapped with and meshed into the others. Some of Cheshire's most important turnpikes were built well into the railway age and remained key arteries of trade and commerce even when paralleled by railway routes.

If we consider the mileage of new turnpike roads, rather than the number of Acts, a broadly similar pattern is revealed. Figure 4 shows the mileage by decade, though it must be emphasised that only mileage within Cheshire is included, and many Acts included long stretches of road beyond the county boundary. The peak decade was the 1780s, during which more than one-fifth of the total Cheshire mileage was authorised, including the largest scheme of all, the turnpiking of the roads from Chester into Wirral. The greatly increased activity in 1750–1770 and 1820–1840 is again apparent.

The emerging county network
By 1760 Acts had been passed for the turnpiking of the trunk roads from Chester to Wrexham, Whitchurch, Nantwich and Newcastle-under-Lyme; from Warrington through Knutsford to Staffordshire; and from Manchester to Buxton and Doncaster. Other Acts had authorised the improvement of connecting roads, so a countywide network was emerging. Thus, when the Cranage-Knutsford-Warrington route was authorised in 1753, the roads from Mere to Bucklow Hill and Altrincham, and from Bucklow Hill to Northwich (the modern A556) were included in the scheme. In the same year the roads from Sandbach via Middlewich to Winsford Bridge and from Middlewich to Northwich were authorised, and in 1759 the road from Macclesfield, over the eastern moors to Buxton, a route with major importance in the history of turnpikes in general (Figure 5).

Key routes turnpiked in the 1760s included that from Leek to Macclesfield and Bullock Smithy,[10] where it joined the Manchester-Buxton turnpike of 1725, together with (by a

Figure 5. The Macclesfield and Buxton turnpike was turnpiked in 1759 using the existing alignment of narrow and often very steep lanes. In the mid-1820s the route was almost completely superseded by a newly-constructed road, leaving the old alignment as country lanes or moorland tracks. This excellently-preserved milestone from the 1759 route stands amid the heather and moor grass close to the old road, north-west of the *Cat and Fiddle* inn.

separate Act) the linking road from Congleton to Leek and Ashbourne. These, with the Macclesfield-Buxton road, provided a main north-south artery through east Cheshire and east-west links from the Cheshire plain into Derbyshire, enhanced in 1769 with the turnpiking of the road from Macclesfield via Chelford and Knutsford to Tabley, joining the road to Northwich. The cross-Pennine traffic was of particular importance, and in the 1760s other routes were added. Two were part of the Woodhead network: roads from Stockport to Saddleworth via Audenshaw and Ashton-under-Lyne, with a branch from Bredbury to Mottram in Longdendale, and in 1768 a turnpike from Huddersfield to Woodhead crossing the formidably bleak terrain of Holme Moss (reaching 1,719 feet above sea level and thus claiming the honours as Cheshire's highest turnpike). In 1770 the Macclesfield-Whaley Bridge road, via Kettleshulme, provided another route into the Peak District – the recognised destinations, shown on milestones, were Chapel-en-le-Frith and Sheffield, emphasising its intended role as an inter-regional artery.

Another network was developing in south-west Cheshire, focusing on Nantwich. The town was already on the main turnpike from Chester to Stone and Lichfield, and in 1766–67 new routes were authorised from Newcastle-under-Lyme and the Potteries to the eastern edge of the town, and from Hinstock near Newport, via Market Drayton. These roads were secondary in status, inter-urban rather than inter-regional, but they and others such as the Wrexham to Malpas road (also 1767) knitted together the already-improved arterial routes, providing alternatives and linking market towns to the developing network. By 1770 about 235 miles of Cheshire road had been authorised (Figure 6).

The impact of the Industrial Revolution

While the historical debate about the Industrial Revolution continues, and the term and concept are regarded with disfavour by some, the notion of an economic take-off in the 1770s and 1780s remains useful. The fourth quarter of the eighteenth century saw industrialisation in north-east Cheshire,

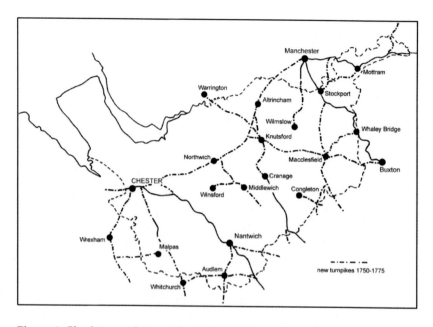

Figure 6. Cheshire roads turnpiked 1750–1775.

associated with the expansion of existing towns such as Macclesfield, Congleton and Stockport, and the emergence of new industrial communities at, for example, Hyde, Dukinfield and Stalybridge. The first indications of suburban growth can also be detected, at Altrincham, Sale and Cheadle which were within easy reach of Manchester. At the opposite end of the county, the Wirral ferries could be used for commuting to Liverpool. Urban growth and industrial development had the potential to generate valuable new business for turnpike roads, especially as the canal network was relatively poorly-developed in much of the region. Road transport was fundamental to industrialisation.

There were therefore twin pressures for further road improvement: from the financial perspective the possibility of substantial profits from tolls was attractive, but more important was the attitude of manufacturers, who saw a better highway infrastructure as an essential prerequisite to, and integral component of, economic growth.[11] Roads could carry coal and building materials, raw materials and finished products for the textile and metal-working industries, food to the growing cities, and of course passenger traffic. During the 1780s and 1790s these imperatives began to play a key role in the promotion of new turnpike schemes in the county, and in the extension of existing roads by means of branches.

A good example is provided by the Act of 1780 which renewed the Macclesfield and Buxton Trust, and also authorised the building of new branches on the lonely moors of the Cheshire-Derbyshire border 'to communicate with certain Coal-pits now or hereafter to be opened upon the Moss called Goits-moss and Thatch Marsh' and to the limestone quarries and kilns on Grin Low south of Buxton. These branch roads would allow 'Coals [to be] conveyed to the said Kilns and Lime carried from thence into the Counties of Chester and Lancaster [to the] great Relief and Advantage to all persons supplied with Lime from the above Kilns'. The coalpits and kilns were already served by the Buxton and Leek turnpike of 1765, but there had been vociferous complaints about the high tolls charged by the latter trust. The 1780 Act specifically states that henceforth traffic to the pits and kilns could move 'without passing on the said Turnpike Road from Leek to Buxton or the branches thereof'.[12] Another instance of a road specifically intended to serve industrial premises occurs in the 1786 Act which authorised the turnpike from Congleton to Buxton and included a short branch to the brass and copper mills on the River Dane at Havannah, while in 1788 the renewal of the powers for the Wrexham-Chester road added a cross-country branch from Rossett to Llay, Cefn-y-bedd and Minera to serve limeworks, coalpits and other industries around Hope and Abermorddu.

In the north east of the county, and adjacent areas of Derbyshire, Yorkshire and Lancashire, the network became increasingly complex. An Act of 1792 authorised the turnpiking of a group of roads from Chapel-en-le-Frith via Hayfield to Glossop and Longdendale, and a year later a route from Saddleworth via Mossley and Stalybridge to Mottram and Glossop. In 1801 the Stockport to Marple Bridge road was turnpiked, together with branches to New Mills and from New Mills to Disley, and two years later this was supplemented by routes from Glossop to Marple Bridge, Compstall (where the Andrews Brothers were developing their model cotton-spinning community), Padfield, Hadfield and Tintwistle. By 1810 a skein of improved roads crossed the Pennine foothills from the Yorkshire border through the Cheshire panhandle to the Goyt Valley and Stockport (Figure 7).

The same period saw much increased connectivity on the secondary routes of mid- and south Cheshire. Between 1780 and 1805 turnpiking was extended to the roads from Wilmslow through Nether Alderley to Congleton and the Potteries; Tarporley to the Weaver Navigation at Acton Bridge (a good example of the complementary nature of modes of transport); Sandbach into Staffordshire; Macclesfield to Congleton; and Holmes Chapel to Chelford. In the north the main road from Newton-by-Chester to Wilderspool Causeway on the edge of Warrington was turnpiked from 1786, together with the secondary link from Frodsham to Ashton Lane Ends near Kelsall, and in 1788 the short road from Vicars Cross to Hoole forming a Chester bypass.

The most important scheme of the 1780s, one of particular interest in terms of the county's social and economic history,

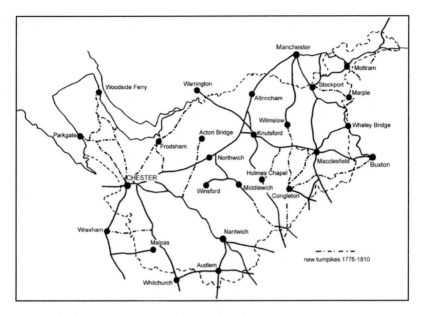

Figure 7. Cheshire roads turnpiked 1775–1810.

was the turnpiking from 1787 of the road from Chester via Bromborough to Woodside Ferry, together with the Chester-Neston-Parkgate road, and the cross-peninsula routes from Neston to Eastham Ferry via Willaston and Hooton, and Neston to Tranmere via Thornton Hough. These were the first turnpikes in Wirral: with a small population, no significant towns, and no industry of any size, the area had not hitherto been promising territory. But the massive growth of Liverpool, and the increasing use of the Wirral ferries – a quicker route over the Mersey than the long detour via Warrington or the hazardous crossing at Runcorn – generated substantial new traffic. The road network was quite inadequate to deal with this, and extensive turnpiking was essential. The inclusion of the road to Parkgate reflects its role as the passenger port for

205

Ireland, although that was not to continue much longer, for in 1815 the last boats were withdrawn as a result of the transfer of ferry services to Holyhead, at the far end of Telford's magnificent turnpike through the mountains of North Wales.[13] The promoters of the Wirral turnpikes were particularly conscious of the Liverpool trade. Not only were the Eastham and Woodside Ferries the destinations of the roads, but the trustees included the mayor and aldermen of the City of Chester, and the mayor, bailiffs and twenty-four senior common councillors of the borough of Liverpool. This civic sponsorship reflected the powerful commercial interests in both cities, for whom the improved communications had much to offer.

From improvement to replacement in East Cheshire

From the late 1780s a new phase of turnpike development exerted a powerful impact upon the landscape of Cheshire. Almost all the roads considered hitherto were ancient highways, where turnpiking entailed better surfacing, draining, fencing or hedging, and signing, together with the construction of tollhouses and gates and the erection of milestones. In some instances widening was also involved and in a few examples, of which the Holme Moss road is perhaps the most impressive, a *de facto* new road was created on what had previously been little more than a moorland track. Such upgradings resulted in far-reaching changes to traffic itself: an Act of 1731 for the Manchester to Buxton turnpike stated that 'the manner of carriage over the said roads was usually by packhorses [but] by the great amendment and widening of the said roads [it] is of late changed into wheeled carriage', the proprietors claiming that as a result toll income was diminished because many fewer animals passed by.[14] In essence, though, the work up to the 1780s was achieved largely by improving existing roads. From the 1740s onwards a few short stretches of new road were built, mainly to cut out particularly awkward bends or narrow sections of village street, but these were secondary to the general task of improving existing alignments.

In 1753, however, a more substantial example of new construction was authorised. The road from Ardwick to Didsbury was turnpiked under the 1731 Act for the Manchester and Buxton road, but southward from Didsbury the ancient route remained unimproved. In 1753 the powers of the trust came up for renewal, and it was proposed to extend the Didsbury branch road into Cheshire to terminate at the bridge over the Bollin at Wilmslow. This, it was noted, was 'the nearest Road from the Market Town of Manchester to London', but it passed 'through a Ford in the River Mersey called Cheadle Ford', the river being 'very broad and rapid [and] upon every little Rise of Water, very difficult and hazardous to pass, and in Time of High Floods impassable'.[15] A bridge was duly built, approached by sections of new road (now the B5095) between Didsbury and Cheadle villages.

In 1764 the concept of building new roads, rather than simply upgrading existing ones, was carried a stage further by substantial changes to the Manchester and Buxton turnpike. Heading eastwards from Whaley Bridge it climbed over 600 feet in less than two miles, as a narrow lane along the ridge of Eccles Pike, before dropping down to Chapel-en-le-Frith. The 1764 Act authorised a major diversion, with a completely new road two and a half miles long following the valley of Randal Carr Brook past Combs village to avoid a section of road 'very mountainous steep and dangerous to Travellers'. That diversion was entirely in Derbyshire, but the Act also authorised the diversion of another section, on the Cheshire side of the boundary from Whaley Bridge to the end of

Longside Common south of Disley,[16] involving a new section of road almost a mile in length, curving gently round the side of the moor instead of crossing the summit.

In the hilly areas east of the Manchester-Macclesfield-Congleton turnpike the roads were usually adaptations of ancient tracks and lanes, with a combination of sharp bends, extreme narrowness, and steep hills that was not a problem for packhorses but presented a formidable challenge to wheeled vehicles. From the middle of the century the volume, size and weight of goods vehicles grew rapidly, as a result of industrialisation. For a heavy cart laden with coal, or bales of cotton cloth, or roofing slabs, the unimproved alignments were a tremendous constraint, even though surfaces and drainage were considerably better than thirty years earlier. The techniques of surfacing, cambering and drainage had been tested over the decades, so the next logical step was to make major alterations to the alignment of roads, with easier gradients, less climbing and, especially, less wasted effort occasioned by steep climbs followed by sharp descents. An even and steady gradient was preferable and that, combined with a standard width and more manageable curves, would produce roads that were much more efficient for the traffic which used them. The experiment in the 1760s with rerouting sections of the Buxton turnpike proved the benefits of that approach, though it inevitably involved additional expenditure on land purchase and construction costs.

The road from Macclesfield to Whaley Bridge via Rainow and Kettleshulme was turnpiked in 1770, a project which occupied 'an intermediate position in turnpike history'. Most of the alignment followed existing lanes, but about one and a half miles on either side of the summit at Charles Head was on a new alignment, curving along the contour and superseding the extremely steep route of the old lane which twice drops down into a deep valley and climbs back again.[17] From 1789 the road between Congleton and Buxton was turnpiked, a scheme which involved more extensive use of new construction. Between Bosley and the Derbyshire border, passing close to Wincle and Wildboarclough (a distance of nine miles) almost all the road was either completely new or a wholesale reconstruction of moorland trackways. The route is now perceived as dangerous, because of the many bends on its sinuous course, but two and a quarter centuries ago it was innovative, meeting the topographical challenge of the deeply dissected hills of the western slopes of the Peak District and the bleak moorland plateau above. At Bosley crossroads the road is 575 feet above sea level, and on the Derbyshire border 1,500 feet, a net gain of 925 feet. It contours sinuously upwards, but in order to cross the valley of the Clough Brook at Allgreave the road is forced to descend, very steeply, 560 feet before climbing again by a series of sharp bends.

That is wasted effort, and the builders of later turnpikes sought to avoid such problems, taking the view that increased distance, obtained by insistence on long contoured stretches around valley sides and the shoulders of hills, was preferable to steepness and futile descent and ascent. Speed in the absolute sense of miles per hour was not a consideration (nothing could go faster than a horse) but overall journey time definitely was, and efficiency of effort was a key element in the equation. In east Cheshire, as in Pennine Lancashire, the West Riding and Derbyshire, the new principles of road construction were adopted not only by the promoters of new turnpikes but also by existing trusts. This was powerfully demonstrated by the 1820 scheme for the rerouting of the Manchester and Buxton turnpike, and the remarkable replacement of the 1759 Macclesfield and Buxton road in the mid-1820s.

As already noted, two sections of the Buxton turnpike were superseded in the 1760s, and in their extension Act of 1820 the trustees obtained powers to make a further series of major changes to the road between Heaton Chapel, north of Stockport, and Whaley Bridge. Some six and a half miles of the eleven-mile stretch of road would be superseded by completely new construction. With greatly increased traffic, and considerations of efficiency and shortened journey times, the existing road was clearly substandard. It passed through the congested centre of Stockport, with steep climbs on either side of the bridge over the Mersey and a very troublesome section through the market place. Between Heaviley and High Lane it passed through open countryside and was relatively easily graded, climbing 300 feet in four and a half miles, but from the east end of High Lane the road climbed 150 feet in half a mile to Jackson's Edge, before dropping no less sharply to Disley village. That was followed by a gruelling ascent to Whaley Moor, a flat stretch of a mile and a half, and then a giddy slope of 300 feet in half a mile down Whaley Lane. This combination of urban congestion at Stockport, and a succession of extremely steep and long hills between High Lane and Whaley Bridge, was particularly difficult because much of the traffic was heavy goods wagons carrying coal, flagstones, lime and gritstone from the Peak District.

The new alignment began with a magnificently engineered bypass west of Stockport town, straights and smooth sweeping curves carrying the broad new road from Heaton Chapel to Heaviley, crossing the Mersey on a high-level bridge approached by massive embankments. Named Wellington Road after the hero of Waterloo, and now the A6, it is the main north-south element in Stockport's road network almost two centuries later. Between High Lane and Whaley Bridge a

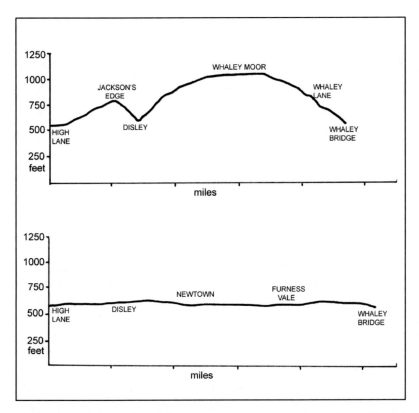

Figure 8. Gradient profile of the old and new turnpikes from Heaton Chapel to Whaley Bridge.

completely new road was built, curving south of Jackson's Edge to cross the old alignment at right angles in the centre of Disley (Plate 10), and then winding along the contour through Newton and Furness Vale. The old route involved a total of almost 600 feet of climbing between High Lane and Whaley: the new route was almost level throughout. It was significantly longer but the advantages of perfect gradients far outweighed that consideration (Figure 8). The road helped to reshape the

211

geography of the Cheshire-Derbyshire border, making the industrialising town of New Mills more accessible, giving improved opportunities to exploit the coal and other resources of this section of the Goyt valley (as at Furness Vale) and, within a decade, opening up the area south of Stockport to suburban development.

The construction work on the Manchester and Buxton turnpike was completed in 1826, by which time work on another great project, the replacement of the Macclesfield and Buxton road, was well advanced. The existing road, turnpiked in 1759, left the south end of Macclesfield town and climbed by an exceptionally steep and narrow lane up the slopes of Blakelow and Tegg's Nose to Walker Barn, before descending into Wildboarclough, climbing again past Torgate, and crawling up the rocky gorge below Stake Farm to the moorland summit at the *Cat and Fiddle*. It then crossed the head of the Goyt valley and ran over the moorland ridge to Buxton. It was steep, narrow and prone to flooding but, as the post-1780 branches to collieries and limeworks emphasised, it was heavily used by industrial traffic and Macclesfield, in particular, relied upon the coal supplies brought down from the Axe Edge moors and Goyts Moss. The route climbed from 480 feet at Macclesfield to a summit of 1,690 feet at the *Cat and Fiddle*. In principle the road involved 1,210 feet of climbing, but such was its up and down course that the actual figure was almost 1,700 feet.

The new road, authorised in 1821, was engineered with exceptional skill. It was almost two miles longer than the 1759 route, but between Macclesfield and the *Cat and Fiddle* there was a mere thirty feet of descent (compared with almost 500 feet on the old road). This was achieved by a strict rule that, whenever possible, the alignment contoured round valleys and ascended slopes at an even gradient. The old and new routes barely coincided: only for a few hundred yards between Walker Barn and Turnshawflat, and again briefly at the summit, do they share alignments, though for considerable stretches they are within sight of each other (Figure 9 and Plate 11). Ironically, the very attribute that made the new road a success – its winding alignment which did not matter at all in the days of horse-drawn vehicles – now makes it notoriously dangerous. A 50 mph speed limit is rigorously imposed throughout the length from Macclesfield to Buxton and the old route, which for the most part remains as a country lane, is heavily-used by motorists avoiding the speed cameras on its 1820s replacement.

New roads were built elsewhere in east Cheshire, not to avoid steep gradients but to provide shorter inter-urban links and bypass congested town centres. Eastwards from Manchester the turnpike of the 1730s followed Ashton Old Road (A635), but this, though direct and straight, was eventually supplemented by other newly-constructed turnpikes: Ashton New Road, from Ancoats via Droylesden, and in 1818 Hyde Road, which ran from Ardwick Green through Denton to the canal bridge at Hyde, most of the route being in arrow-straight alignments which slashed across the grain of the landscape. In 1833 the Hyde road was extended, again as completely new construction, from Hyde, via Godley and Hattersley, to Mottram in Longdendale. This road is now built-up along almost its entire length but when built in 1818 and 1833 it cut across open countryside, linking fast-growing industrial communities. It reduced the length of road from Manchester to Mottram by almost two miles and was far superior in quality to the old route: within a generation it had become the main road to Yorkshire (Figure 10).

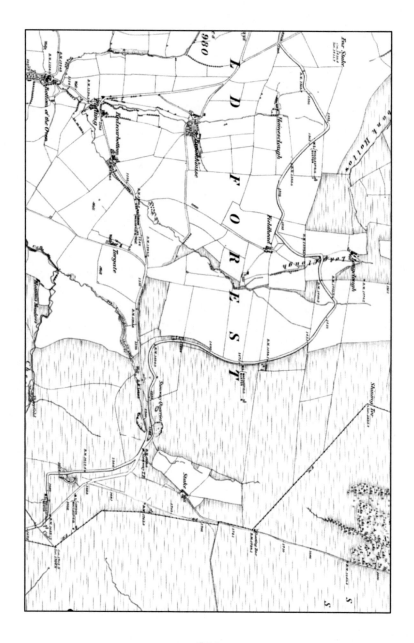

Completing the network in central and western Cheshire
In the rest of Cheshire the period from 1800 to the 1830s saw many gaps filled by smaller locally promoted projects for turnpiking existing roads (Figure 11). Schemes such as Nantwich-Crewe-Sandbach (1816), Sandbach to Congleton (1835) and Nantwich to Middlewich and Congleton (also 1835) greatly increased connectivity and gave south Cheshire a turnpike network almost unequalled in its comprehensive coverage of key routes and market towns. In north Cheshire the commercial and economic imperative was fuelled by coal, salt and other industrial products and by the rise of manufacturing towns along the Mersey valley from Stockport to the sea.[18] A key route was from Stockport through Cheadle, Altrincham and Lymm to Warrington, providing a high-quality road along the Cheshire side of the river authorised in 1820, and in 1829 extended by the road from Grappenhall to the Frodsham turnpike at Lower Walton, bypassing Warrington and providing a much-improved link from Stockport to Chester. Other roads in the Cheshire plain were upgraded, though not as comprehensively as the hill roads in the east. Some of these changes were specifically authorised by parliamentary Act. Thus in 1808 an Act authorised a new one and a half mile stretch of the Macclesfield-Knutsford road at Henbury,

Figure 9 (left). The old and new turnpikes from Macclesfield to Buxton, shown on the first edition 6-inch map of 1870. The 1759 turnpike runs east past Platting and Redscarbottom and then across the moorland towards the *Cat and Fiddle*. The only clear indication that it was a turnpike are the two milestones shown along its route. At Stonway it intersects the 1821 road, which is distinguished by its winding but evenly graded alignment, climbing steadily past Fieldhead towards the summit. A tollbar (marked as 'Stonway TP', or turnpike) was carefully placed where the two routes very briefly coincided so that the travellers could not avoid payment on the new road by diverting down the old.

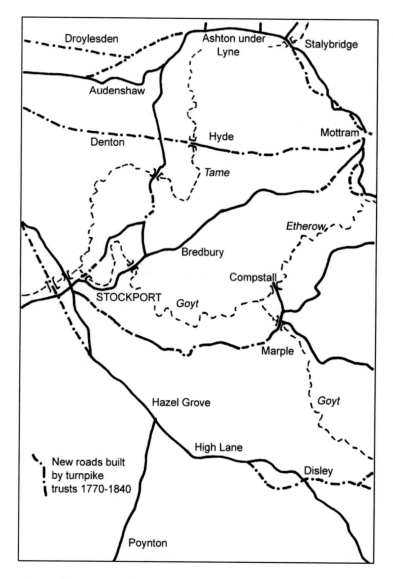

Figure 10. New turnpike road construction in north-east Cheshire.

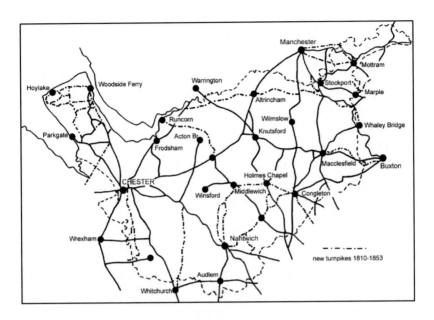

Figure 11. Cheshire roads turnpiked 1810–1853.

bypassing back lanes through Birtles which were said to be 'in many Places very narrow, hilly, and incommodious to Travellers', and in 1830 the difficult stretch of the road from Chester to Northwich at Kelsall was improved by the building of a diversion that avoided a narrow hill, while a section of the Nantwich road at Duddon was also diverted. Others, however, were the subject of local decisions of the trustees, as in 1824 when an agreement was made between John Goff of Carden, 'roadmaker', and the trustees of the Chester and Whitchurch turnpike, to build a new road from Duckington Dingle across Hampton Heath to No Man's Heath, a distance of three and a half miles. The old road survives as a minor lane up to three quarters of a mile east of the present (1824) alignment of the A41, passing through the significantly-named Ashtons Cross and Hampton Post.[19]

The final phase of turnpike development in the county, during the reign of William IV and into that of Victoria, focused particularly on Wirral. Here there were features which have national significance in the history of road development. As noted, the roads from Chester to Parkgate and to Woodside Ferry, and the cross-routes from Neston to Woodside and Eastham Ferry, were turnpiked from 1787, but the meandering alignments of existing roads were adopted. As traffic and population grew with the commercial and business expansion of Liverpool these indirect routes were increasingly inadequate, but from the mid-1820s a new factor entered consideration: the founding and meteoric rise of Birkenhead as a new town, port and industrial centre. In 1820 there was a short diversion of the Woodside turnpike in Tranmere, but more ambitious projects followed. An Act of 1833 authorised the extensive reconstruction of the turnpike between Chester and Birkenhead, involving a completely new arterial road from Tranmere past Rock Ferry to Bromborough, cutting out the indirect inland route through Bebington. The new road had considerable engineering works, as it crossed the low-lying marshy ground and tidal inlets of the Mersey shore. One of those working on the project was the Cheshire-born engineer Thomas Brassey: this was the first major contract undertaken by the man destined to become the greatest railway builder in the world. There were other diversions, such as the short bypass of Great Sutton village, and a new road from Brimstage Lane to Lower Bebington and Spital. The impact of these changes was far-reaching, because the new road opened up the riverside marshes to industrial development at New Ferry, Rock Ferry and Bromborough Pool.

Meanwhile, a remarkable development was taking place at the northern end of Wirral. An Act of 1828 authorised a complex network of turnpike roads: the inland route from

Neston to Hoylake; a branch from Upton to Woodside Ferry; and others from Arrow House to Greasby, Frankby and Grange, from Arrow House to Prenton and Birkenhead, and from Prenton to Tranmere. Essentially, the scheme involved a spine road up the peninsula to Hoylake, and east-west roads from the ferries on the Mersey shore to the communities on the Dee shore, via the rural villages in the interior. In 1841 a further Act added the road from Woodside to Meols via Bidston and Moreton. Both the 1828 and 1841 schemes, which totalled thirty-seven miles, included sections of new road which provided short-cuts between the winding country lanes around which the design was based.

The territory through which the roads passed was unlike that of any previous turnpike project in Cheshire and, indeed, was scarcely matched anywhere else in England. It was thinly-populated and almost entirely agricultural, with no major urban centre and no industries and, by definition, not en route to anywhere else. The Act for the 1828 scheme hints at the rationale for turnpiking thirty-seven miles of country roads: the scheme would 'be a great Advantage and Convenience to the Owners and Occupiers of Estates and Residents within the several Places and Districts through which the said Roads will pass, and other Inhabitants of the adjacent Country'.[20] In other words, this pair of turnpike schemes was designed for passenger traffic, to create commuter traffic between the incipient dormitory villages of rural Wirral, the Mersey ferries and the growing town of Birkenhead. Businessmen could live in suburban or rural peace and travel by carriage to the ferries or the new industrial areas on the Mersey shore. Other turnpikes became important for commuters: in Cheshire, for example, the early nineteenth-century growth of Altrincham, Wilmslow, Cheadle and Hazel Grove was fostered by road transport on the turnpike roads radiating south from Manchester, and substantially predated railway commuting. But the Wirral turnpikes of 1828 and 1841 were developed primarily for that purpose: the passenger traffic was not an incidental bonus, but was the *raison d'être* of the project. Had the development of turnpikes not been stunted by the growth of railways in the 1840s and 1850s, a new generation of toll roads designed for passenger traffic would almost certainly have developed in the hinterlands of major towns and cities. The Wirral examples were a harbinger of what might have happened much more widely.

In 1827 an Act was passed for a turnpike along the south bank of the Dee from Flint via Connah's Quay to the King's Ferry at Shotton, and three years later another Act authorised a road from the Chester-Parkgate road at Woodbank to the north end of the ferry, with a matching road on the south side connecting with the Wrexham-North Wales turnpike at Northop. The 1830 Act was not implemented, being superseded by an Act of 1835 which authorised a broadly similar road and was itself repealed by another Act in 1838. The 1830 and 1835 schemes had involved a modest branch road linking to the ferry over the Dee and complemented by small schemes on the Welsh side. In 1838, though, something much more ambitious was envisaged – an arterial highway which in its scale, specifications and landscape impact bore a closer relationship to the new roads of the 1920s than to the great majority of existing turnpikes. Although its promoters probably drew inspiration from the purpose-built turnpikes in, for example, east Cheshire (such as the Manchester to Hyde road of 1818) they went beyond this in visualising an inter-regional highway, an artery of commerce, trade and passenger traffic.

The project, implemented in the early 1840s, involved a road from Hooton Grange on the Woodside-Chester turnpike across the flat farmland of south Wirral, to the King's Ferry. It was deliberately designed for speed: although horses still provided the only means of haulage, this road was constructed of long straights, linked by the slightest of bends. It avoided all settlements, and was 50 feet wide, almost twice the standard width for a 'traditional' turnpike road. Like its progenitors in east Cheshire, it disregarded the constraints of landscape, slicing through fields and lanes without reference to field boundaries or the existing network of lanes. Topographical constraints were few, but where there were valleys (as at Shotwick) the road was carried across on a massive embankment. The aim was clear: the road provided a very direct route from Liverpool to North Wales, substantially reducing the length of the journey. From Birkenhead to Mold by the existing turnpike, through the streets of Chester, was twenty six miles, but the new road reduced the distance to twenty miles, mostly on open roads. The ferry (renamed Queensferry in honour of the new monarch) was a problem, although the intention (eventually realised in 1893) was to build a bridge.

This was not the last turnpike road in Cheshire. In 1848 the road from Gorsty Hill, on the Staffordshire border east of Nantwich, to Crewe Station was turnpiked, with a completely new section of almost two miles. The old road from Weston to Crewe Green ran through the grounds of Crewe Hall, and the Nantwich and Wheelock Trust came to an arrangement with Lord Crewe to build the new and more direct road south of the park, a strategy which cost them dear as the agreement was followed by a decade and a half of litigation.[21] The significance of this road in terms of turnpike history is the link to the station. Active trustees, those with more vision, recognised that at least in principle there was potential traffic to be derived from serving stations. Such strategies might help to meet the challenge which the railway posed, and for a time the new road at Crewe did indeed attract coach traffic. But the expansion of the railway network eventually put paid to that, and by the 1860s the road was earning only small amounts from tolls.

Finally, in 1853, came the turnpiking of the road from Chester to Shocklach and Worthenbury, with a branch from Churton to Farndon.[22] This road, particularly late by national standards, passed through a purely agricultural landscape, following a winding alignment through a string of small villages to a remote junction with the Bangor on Dee-Malpas turnpike. It is very difficult to see how such a road could ever have been profitable, apart from the rather remote possibility of abstracting traffic from the Chester-Wrexham and Chester-Whitchurch roads. In contrast to the ambitious schemes of the 1830s and 1840s this was a very traditional scheme involving almost no improvement other than the customary surfacing, draining and signing. Cheshire's last turnpike was also its most rural. Despite the absence of any competing railway branch it was never viable, and in 1871 was amalgamated with the parallel Whitchurch Trust, the joint body itself being wound up only six years later. The Farndon and Shocklach road had been a turnpike for little more than twenty years.

Conclusion

In the final three decades of turnpike development in the county we see innovative types of road promotion and development. The first, exemplified by the post-1828 network in north Wirral, was the creation of turnpikes particularly designed for passenger traffic, to carry commuters and to cater for the growing number of middle-class residents. The second, demonstrated by the 1818 and 1833 construction of the arterial road from Manchester via Hyde to Mottram, and the even more remarkable road from Hooton to Queensferry, was the building of new inter-urban and inter-regional highways, designed to maximise efficiency of transport by minimising distance and avoiding built-up areas. The third, exemplified by the Macclesfield-Buxton new road and the rerouting of the Manchester-Buxton road, both carried out in the 1820s, used sophisticated planning and engineering principles to develop roads in hill country with gradients as even and gradual as possible (at the expense of distance). The fourth was the recognition that railway stations might perhaps represent a valuable source of traffic in the future.

The fate of the turnpike network is instructive. The entire system was dismantled in the 1870s and 1880s, as powers for existing trusts lapsed. The trusts themselves were dissolved, and their assets returned to local authority control. In Cheshire the county council, which came into being on 1 January 1889, inherited an outstandingly good network of inter-urban roads which were almost without exception former turnpikes. It continued their work, including that of providing mileposts (usually of cast-iron) proudly bearing its own name. Less than fifty years after the final trust was established, and only fifteen years after the last trusts were wound up, the motor age began, and roads entered a new and profoundly different phase in their history. It is intriguing to speculate about what would have happened if the demise of the trusts had been slower. If they had managed to survive into the Edwardian period, as was by no means impossible, the entire basis of road administration and road funding in Britain would have been radically different from that which emerged in the 1920s and 1930s. The existence of a ready-made national system of toll roads, continuing that which the trusts had so effectively operated for a century and a half, would have rendered redundant the current contentious debate about road pricing.

The landscape of Cheshire was changed in many ways by the work of the turnpike trusts. Driving down the main road from Buxton to Macclesfield we follow a superb engineering project of the 1820s, from the sharp bends but even gradients on the high moors to the long straight mile into central Macclesfield. Going south from Birkenhead, along the broad, direct and extremely busy New Chester Road, we use the infrastructure created by Thomas Brassey in the 1830s, as his engineering talents transformed the Wirral shore. Heading east from Mottram in Longdendale, through poor Tintwistle, racked by incessant traffic, and up the long bends past Crowden and Woodhead to the Yorkshire border, we follow one of England's earliest inter-urban road projects, which at the beginning of the 1730s reshaped and remodelled an ancient track that in places was little more than a packhorse route. And if we go from Hooton towards the bridge at Queensferry, along that impressively straight highway, we traverse a road of the early 1840s which, foreshadowing the much more celebrated motor roads of the 1920s, was in its way as revolutionary as the railways with which it was in competition.

References
1. It is impossible to produce an exact figure, as some short sections of authorised route were never in fact turnpiked and some diversions were constructed without separate parliamentary approval. The figure given here represents the best estimate.
2. I should like particularly to thank K. Lawrence for allowing me access to his important unpublished paper, 'The turnpike roads to Nantwich'. It discusses these aspects of

local turnpikes in detail and special attention is given to tolls, traffic levels and the financial management of individual trusts.

3. A.G. Crosby, 'The regional road network and the growth of Manchester in the sixteenth and seventeenth centuries', *Manchester Region History Review*, XIX (2008), 1–16.

4. The town of Stalybridge did not exist in 1731.

5. Preamble to the Act for the Lawton-Cranage road, 4 Geo. II c.3 (1730).

6. Preamble to the Act for the Doncaster-Saltersbrook road, 14 Geo. II c.31 (1741).

7. This included Hatton to Barnhill, turnpiked in 1705, the powers for which had lapsed in 1729.

8. The earliest work on turnpikes in the region was published by W. Harrison, 'The development of the turnpike system in Lancashire and Cheshire', *THSLC*, IV (1886) and X (1892). This was pioneering research not just locally but nationally. The best-known general work is W. Albert, *The Turnpike Road System in England 1663-1840* (Cambridge, 1972) but this is in some ways unsatisfactory. The list of turnpike Acts is not reliable and the cut-off date (1840) is too early. Cheshire is largely ignored, and the index includes the memorable entry 'Macclesfield: see Sheffield'.

9. For the chronology and geography of Lancashire turnpikes see J. Whiteley, 'The turnpike era' in A.G. Crosby, ed., *Leading the Way: A History of Lancashire's Roads* (Preston, 1998), 119–82.

10. In 1836 Bullock Smithy was renamed Hazel Grove, as this was felt to be more suitable for a respectable suburb: a name which was fostered not by the railway, but by the turnpike road, now the A6.

11. For the most recent discussion of this crucial aspect see R. Hart and G. Timmins, 'Lancashire's highway men: the business community and road improvements during the industrial revolution', *Manchester Region History Review*, XXI (2010), 128–43.

12. Quotations from the Macclesfield and Buxton turnpike Act, 20 Geo. III c.91 (1780).

13. The history of the road links to Parkgate is explained in G. Place, *The Rise and Fall of Parkgate, Passenger Port for Ireland, 1686–1815* (Chetham Soc., 3rd ser, 1994), 231–40.

14. For the pre-turnpike traffic and routeways of the Peak District (including the moorland ridges on the borders of Cheshire and Derbyshire) see D. Hey, *Packmen, Carriers and Packhorse Roads: Trade and Communications in North Derbyshire and South Yorkshire* (Leicester, 1980), especially chapters 1 and 4.

15. Preamble to the Manchester and Buxton turnpike Act, 26 Geo. II c.53 (1753).

16. Quotations taken from the Manchester and Buxton turnpike Act, 4 Geo. III c.45 (1764).

17. G. Longden, *Kerridge Ridge and Ingersley Vale: A Historical Study* (prepared 2002). Available: <<http://www.kriv.org.uk/documents/historical-study.pdf>>.

18. For a closely-argued paper which discusses traffic by different transport modes in north-west Cheshire in the late-1820s, and assesses the problems in measuring traffic volumes, see J. Herson, 'Estimating traffic: a case-study of the Chester sub-region in 1827–28', *Journal of Transport History*, XXIX (2002), 113–46. Available: <<http://www.manchesteruniversitypress.co.uk/uploads/docs/230113.pdf>>.

19. Articles of agreement between Goff and the trustees: CALS: ZTRT/7/7a.

20. Preamble to the Act for the Wirral turnpikes, 7 Geo. IV c.19 (1828).
21. This is discussed in detail in Lawrence, 'The turnpike roads to Nantwich', 26–30.
22. The Chester and Farndon turnpike was authorised by 17 and 18 Vic. c.87.

8

AN EAST CHESHIRE TOWNSHIP IN TRANSITION: THE EARLY INDUSTRIAL LANDSCAPE OF BOLLINGTON

Tom Swailes

Introduction

Bollington is a picturesque town in the gap made by the River Dean valley through the first range of hills at the eastern edge of the Cheshire plain. Part of the ancient Parish of Prestbury, Bollington includes the hamlet of Kerridge and is within the bounds of the former royal manor and forest of Macclesfield. Visitors today can stand in the heart of the town on the former railway viaduct and look across the amphitheatre-like space of the recreation ground to the huge canal embankment and aqueduct beyond (Figure 1). Prominent in the view are stone built workers' cottages and huge steam-powered cotton mills

Figure 1. Bollington Recreation Ground, 1903. The view east from the Bollington viaduct with Clarence Mill to the left and the canal aqueduct to the right.

228

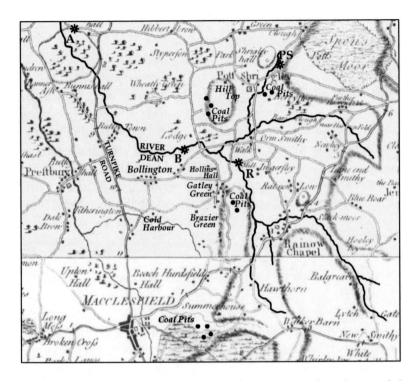

Figure 2. Bollington in 1777. An extract from P.P. Burdett, *Survey of the County Palatine of Chester* (1777), showing the corn mills at Adlington (A), Bollington (B), Rainow and Pott Shrigley (PS) and also showing the local coal pits.

with tall chimneys. All this is the legacy of a bustling industrial landscape. Burdett's 1777 county map shows only a few hamlets within the area of Bollington township, two water mills and some coal pits, but a town grew over the following century: first with the development of mines, quarries and cotton mills, then with connection to the canal and railway networks (Figure 2).[1] This paper considers some physical and documentary evidence for the landscape of early extractive and water-powered industries and for later changes brought about by regional transport infrastructure.

Stone
The lower coal measures of the carboniferous period form the bedrock beneath east Bollington and Kerridge. Dipping or sloping gradually from east to west these strata include evenly bedded 'Kerridge' stone ideal for splitting into slabs for paving and for roofing slates. Parts of Kerridge hill are capped with a relatively soft grit stone, much of which was used for building the boundary ridge wall that separates Bollington from Rainow. In 1810 William Marriott the vicar of Disley described 'an almost rectilinear fence of stone' along the top of Kerridge hill, 'falling down the steep brow of the northern end ... At the bottom of the hill the fence becomes confused amongst the hedges'.[2]

The earliest known map showing Bollington in the forest of Macclesfield indicates 'slate pitts' on the Bollington side of Kerridge hill.[3] The map is undated but a second map in the series bears the date 1611.[4] Walkers on the Gritstone Trail footpath along the top of Kerridge hill can see evidence of old workings, some of which are likely to date from the seventeenth century and earlier (Figure 3). The manuscript survey report, contemporary with the forest maps, refers to 'certaine quarries of stone' and to 'diverse slate pitts', forming part of the commons on 'Kayridge' leased by Bollington township to the mayor, burgesses and other persons in Macclesfield.[5] Such common grounds were treeless: the term forest refers to a royal hunting ground in which development was controlled to preserve the king's game. The only other quarries or 'stone delfes' in the forest were in Rainow township and were also leased to the borough of Macclesfield, at Billinge and at 'Ranowe', presumed to be Rainow Low. Bollington in

Figure 3. Stone Pits on Kerridge hill. The present day view into Rainow from the modern Gritstone Trail, looking from Bollington across the dry stone boundary wall. A line of old stone pits is visible across the centre of the picture.

the early seventeenth century seems to have been of less economic significance than neighbouring Rainow, which was largely under the control of the powerful earls of Derby.[6]

Burdett's map of 1777 names the hamlets of Brazier Green and Gatley Green to the west of Kerridge hill. These settlement names, no longer in use, were probably called after local quarrying families. A will dating from 1683 reveals a John Gatley as executor to Bollington stone mason John Brasier.[7] An eighteenth-century agreement sheds some light on early arrangements for quarrying in the area: Bollingtonians Francis Gatley, a mason, and Henry Bann and Thomas Taylor, husbandmen, contracted with landowner Edward Downes of Worth for quarrying rights at £4 5s a year on the Hardings estate in the northern part of Rainow township.[8] The men agreed to 'work down the said stone pitts in workmanlike manner, down to the Bottom' and were entitled 'to carry off with horses and carts and wanes the stone that shall be gotten

231

in the aforesd stone pits'. It was stipulated that no more than three men were to work the stone pits at one time. This was extractive industry on a small scale, with farmers also turning their hands to quarrying. Quarrying was a useful source of revenue for an estate, although a small one in comparison with agriculture. An estate advertised for sale in 1752 included a property in Macclesfield and three tenanted farms in Bollington, Hurdsfield and Rainow together yielding rents of just over £100 per year, with coal works let at £12 10s a year and stone pits at £3 per year.[9]

William Clayton bought the Endon Estate to the west of Kerridge hill in 1829, just before the opening of the Macclesfield Canal. A coal master with interests in collieries in Lancashire and also at Poynton a few miles north along the canal, Clayton had inherited a share in Swanscoe colliery adjacent to the Endon estate.[10] From the Endon quarries he built a tramway down to the canal in the mid-1830s. From Clayton's stone wharf 'the beautiful white freestone of Kerridge' was shipped out for the construction of new churches and other buildings across east Cheshire and into Lancashire.[11] Clayton's successors continued to find a market in the region for Kerridge stone and some quarries remain in production today.

Coal
Beneath the Kerridge stone lie four workable coal seams separated by shales and mudstones, the continuity of the layers being disrupted by geological faults. The principal east Cheshire fault is the Red Rock Fault with a vertical displacement or throw of over 600 feet. Victorian geologist Edward Hull gave a concise description:

West of the village of Bollington we find the Pebble Beds of the New Red Sandstone on one side of the fault and the hard grits of the Lower Coal-measures on the other. A section in the former occurs in the river bank west of the [Bollington] canal aqueduct, and quarries have been opened in the latter on both sides of the river, as the grit yields a valuable building stone.[12]

West of the Red Rock Fault any coal was too deep to be of interest to early miners. The most easily accessible coal occurred towards the edges of Bollington township, near or across the boundaries with Adlington, Rainow and Hurdsfield. Property for sale in 1779 included a parcel of land in Bollington called the Bottoms, 'lying up to Rainow Mill, in which there is a valuable Coal Mine'.[13] Early mines were generally small-scale operations worked intermittently by a small number of men and boys.[14] Documentary evidence for the early workings is lacking, but there is much evidence on the ground of old bell-pits, shafts, spoil heaps and drifts (Figure 4). In 1795 Dr John Aikin remarked that 'the township of Bollington has a very large steam engine belonging to a coal pit'.[15] The location of that engine is unknown, although field-names on the tithe map indicate several possible sites.

Unlike the Kerridge stone quarries, the Bollington coal mines were not the only suppliers of a valuable commodity. The local collieries were small in size, worked from an early date to supply local demand and inefficient compared to those at Poynton. The canal carried coal into Bollington, rather than carrying it out. A turret or tower on Windmill Lane in Kerridge bearing William Clayton's initials is believed to have been built as a mine engine chimney about 1844 but from an internal inspection it seems never to have been used (Plate 12). Clayton's death in 1851 marked the end of any ambitions to expand coal mining operations in Bollington.

Figure 4. Coal Pits in East Bollington. The present day view across east Bollington from the lower slopes at the north end of Kerridge hill. The two approximately circular platforms either side of the foreground dry stone wall are old coal pits.

Textiles

Mills by the River Dean and by its feeder streams from Pott Shrigley and Rainow were the first very large stone masonry buildings in Bollington, probably at first fitted out with water-frames for cotton spinning on Richard Arkwright's principle. Peter Lomas established the Waterhouse cotton mill in the early

1790s while his brother Elias ran the adjacent tannery.[16] The mill was immediately upstream of the Bollington corn mill, towards the west end of Bollington. The tannery bark house contained what in 1795 Dr John Aikin described as 'a curious water machine for grinding bark'. A large-scale plan of the Waterhouse estate of 1865 shows the tan yard croft downstream of the mill.[17]

In 1806 Bollington joiner and carpenter John Oldham gave evidence that Waterhouse Mill had been built about sixteen years previously and had since been burnt down and rebuilt.[18] From newspaper reports we know that the fire occurred in November 1800.[19] Oldham stated that from about 1792 he was 'employed constantly in working at the Cotton Manufactories and Works which have been erected on the two branches of the River [the Dean] flowing thro' Bollington from Pott [Shrigley] and Rainow'. The flurry of water-powered industrial activity that gave Oldham and many incomers employment in Bollington was to the detriment of the ancient corn mill at Adlington a few miles downstream. In 1807 the representative of Mr Legh of Adlington Hall wrote that 'the water did not come at all into Adlington Mill Pond on Sunday 30th nor on Monday 31st August til 12 o'clock at noon owing to its being held up in the Ponds of the different factories in Bollington'.[20]

The flow of water in the River Dean is generally modest. To supply water to a wheel to drive the machinery in a large factory for the length of a working shift, especially in dry spells, a large storage reservoir was needed. While a reservoir was slowly filling, the water was held up and mills downstream were unable to work unless their reservoirs were already full or they had an alternative form of power. The Waterhouse mill when first built was supplied by water in a sough or trench and only several years later a reservoir was added, presumably due to the increase in demand for water by mills upstream.

According to Oldham the reservoir had at different times been enlarged, particularly in the summer of 1805. Rainow millwright William Richardson reported in 1806 that the reservoir held back the stream no more than a day in the dry season, provided a head or height of water above the wheel of 3 feet and fed a waterwheel of 23 feet diameter.[21]

Information from the statements of Oldham and Richardson combined provides a picture of the water-powered cotton mills of Bollington at the beginning of the early nineteenth century. Some of the mills are named and further information is given in George Longden's historical studies of the area.[22] No stretch of the River Dean went unused. Upstream from Waterhouse Mill was Defiance Mill, built about 1798, with a small reservoir providing a head of water of 3 feet to turn an 18 feet diameter wheel. A large reservoir infilled in 1854 and now the location of Pool Bank car park was associated with Defiance Mill but may also have stored water for other mills much further downstream. Next upstream was Oak Bank Mill, built about 1784 and almost certainly one of the two 'Arkwright' mills referred to in Colquhoun's survey. Associated with this mill were two reservoirs: a small one close to the factory and a much larger one, able to hold the water back for a week and turning a wheel of 20 feet diameter.

Further upstream the Dean is fed by streams from Pott Shrigley and from Rainow. Sowcar Mill on the Pott Shrigley stream was built about 1802, but destroyed by fire in 1841. Richardson described a large reservoir capable of holding the stream back for three days and providing a 3 feet head of water to turn a large wheel of 27 feet diameter. By Oldham's account the water from the reservoir was habitually released to turn the wheel at 6 o'clock in the morning and the Lomas works at Waterhouse Mill being last in line downstream could not generally begin until two hours later. Even Sowcar Mill as first

Figure 5. Bollington Mills. A view showing the mills of east Bollington, engraved sometime after the mid-1830s.

in the queue for water had a 12 horse-power steam engine to keep the factory at work during dry spells.

First upstream on the Rainow tributary was Lower Mill, built about 1792, with a small reservoir and waterwheel of 14 feet diameter. Next upstream was Higher Mill, built about 1789, with a large reservoir able to hold the water back for two days and providing a head of 3 feet to turn a wheel of 19 feet. Lower Mill and Higher Mill were together known as Bollington Mills (Figure 5). Next upstream was Rainow Mill, an old paper mill converted to a cotton factory. The mill weir is inscribed with the partners' initials LPW and WW and with the date 1801. The death of partner William Watts in October 1806 was shocking enough to make national news: 'having occasion to look at the water wheel of a neighbouring mill, the wheel caught him, and he was literally crushed to atoms'.[23] Upstream from Rainow Mill was Ingersley Mill, built about 1793 with a small reservoir, but extended a few years later with a large reservoir about 1 kilometre upstream. The reservoir is now silted up behind a very fine weir built at the top of a natural rock waterfall or cascade. The weir includes a stone inscribed with the initials of the owner Edward Collier and the date 1800. From this reservoir a goit or artificial channel follows the contour along the valley side to supply a wheel tower via a cast iron aqueduct. According to Richardson, there were two waterwheels, an upper wheel of 22 feet diameter discharging water into a lower wheel of 32 feet diameter. These two wheels, presumably timber-framed, were later replaced with a very large wrought iron suspension wheel of 56 feet diameter. The Ingersley Mill reservoir could hold the water for three days and this together with a supplementary steam engine of 18 horse power ensured that the smooth running of the factory was not disrupted by the workings of the several other water-powered mills further upstream in Rainow.

Bryant's county map of 1831 marks most of the mill reservoirs including that at 'Lower House', a cotton mill built downstream from Waterhouse Mill as the last of Bollington's water-powered factories (Figure 6).[24] Lowerhouse Mill was the first 'fireproof' Bollington factory, with floors laid over incombustible shallow masonry arches resting on an internal framing of cast iron beams and columns. Earlier mills had timber floors to large open plan rooms over several storeys, a form of construction that proved vulnerable to fire, particularly when associated with combustible cotton dust and night shift work lit by candle or gaslight. Destruction by fire was a fate suffered by a very significant number of mills nationally.

Transport
Bryant's map also shows the recently completed Macclesfield Canal, before which local industry had been entirely dependent on roads. Heavily laden carts and wains (two axle agricultural

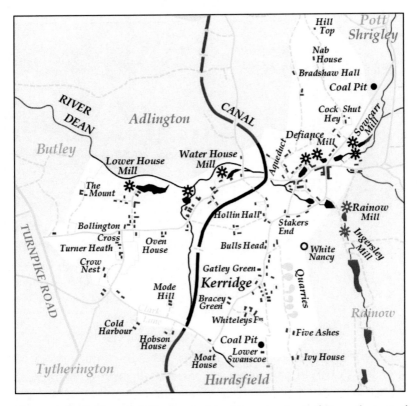

Figure 6. Bollington in 1831. A map based on an extract of Bryant's map of the county surveyed between 1829 and 1831. The density of industrial development was such that Bryant was unable to show all the mills by then built in east Bollington.

wagons pulled by oxen or horses) rutted the steep and imperfectly made local roads, exposing the ground to erosion by surface water run-off. Bollington has several examples of deep hollow-ways so formed. Stone and coal from both Pott Shrigley and Rainow came through Bollington, in the eighteenth century principally en route to Macclesfield. The transport of bulk materials by road changed little before the

Figure 7. Palmerston Street, Bollington, about 1912. The road is substantially built up in front of the Congregational Church with a gentle gradient to suit local quarry and mine traffic. The Memorial Gardens now occupy the foreground space.

advent of the motor vehicle. An eighteenth-century description of the Pott Shrigley roads as 'narrow, ill-formed, inconvenient and gone to decay' reflects their inadequacy for local trade, although problems were sometimes dealt with through local initiatives.[25] For example, one of the overseers for highways in Pott Shrigley was landowner Edward Downes whose property included a quarry to the north of Bollington. A draft contract for the construction of a stretch of road to carry traffic from the quarry specified a width of 24 feet, with 18 inches of beaten stone at the crown cambering to a thickness of 12 inches at the edges. Over a stretch of low ground the road was to be embanked to a height of 3 feet to limit the gradient to 1 in 12 or less. At cuttings a 'good durable breast work of stone' or retaining wall was to be provided and 'made after the same form as the breast work of the Turnpike Road near Mr

Brookbank's house in Tytherington'. In Bollington township itself are several long straight sections of roads built up to give the gentle gradients demanded for the movement of very heavy loads (Figure 7). Such loads included stone memorial slabs weighing a third of a ton and more, quarried on Kerridge for Prestbury and Macclesfield churchyards.

As for water-borne transport, it was claimed for the first Macclesfield canal scheme in 1765 that transport costs would be reduced by half for 'flag, slate and stone, from Stiperson, Alderney and Keyrridge'.[26] For a scheme presented thirty years later the civil engineer Benjamin Outram estimated an annual traffic on the whole canal of 40,000 tons of lime from Derbyshire, 30,000 tons of stone for various purposes and 80,000 tons of coal.[27] In 1811, Thomas Brown, civil engineer, surveyor and coal master of Disley, directed a survey for the line of a canal from Marple, passing through Poynton, Bollington and Macclesfield.[28] When the canal was built in the late 1820s it followed the 1811 line through Bollington township. Brown was a member of the canal management committee and acted as a local engineering consultant; the resident engineer under civil engineer Thomas Telford was William Crosley. The major structures on the canal were the great embankment and aqueduct that separate east from west Bollington. In December 1829 Crosley wrote to Telford offering 'a few observations which have occurred to Mr Brown and me relative to the execution of the work'.[29] A culvert built to take the River Dean beneath the embankment had shifted and the remedy to which Telford had agreed was to infill the culvert and to drive in its stead a tunnel for the river through the bedrock of the valley side. Telford having expressed no preference, a local decision was made to cut the tunnel through the south side, negotiation being required with only two landowners, one of whom was owner of the mill downstream.

Figure 8. The River Dean about 1914, beside Bollington Recreation Ground. A small footbridge crosses the mill goit, and in the background is a coal incline on the canal embankment. Sometime after this picture was taken the river channel was straightened out and the mill goit filled in.

The goit to the mill was culverted through the canal embankment and signs of it are still visible downstream, alongside the recreation ground and on past the railway viaduct (Figure 8).

The availability of relatively cheap coal brought by canal freed the cotton industry from dependency on water for power. Three new canal-side cotton mills were built in Bollington worked by steam engines with coal-fired boilers. The 'fireproof' Clarence and Adelphi mills that dominate the skyline today are described in some detail in the Royal Commission on Historical Monuments volume on east Cheshire textile mills.[30] A third mill, Beehive Mill, was demolished in the twentieth century. Supplementary steam engines were also added to existing water-powered mills, for example at Lowerhouse Mill, about 1835.[31] In November 1835 the management committee of the

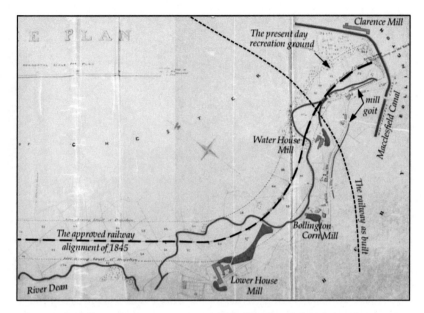

Figure 9. Bollington Railway. A plan based upon an extract from the plan for the unbuilt Bollington branch line of 1845 (CALS: QDP 227), and showing also the present day line of the railway viaduct across the valley of the River Dean.

canal company ordered that 'Mr Oliver & Mr Swindells & others [cotton manufacturers] be authorised to have coal shoots down the embankment at Bollington … the Committee being at liberty to put an end to the privilege on giving a fortnights notice'.[32] The coal chutes can be seen in old photographs and presumably remained in use as long as the mill engines worked.

The railway to Macclesfield was first opened in November 1845 as a Manchester and Birmingham Railway branch line from Cheadle Hulme.[33] A proposal received parliamentary assent on 25 June 1846 for a subsidiary branch to Bollington from the Macclesfield branch line south of Adlington. After

243

Figure 10. The Bollington Railway Viaduct and Waterhouse Mill. The viaduct carried the railway (now the Middlewood Way) on a north to south alignment past the now-demolished mill.

passing Lowerhouse Mill and Waterhouse Mill, the railway would have crossed the open space that is now Bollington recreation ground to a terminal station at the west side of the canal embankment (Figure 9).[34] This line would have provided a direct connection to Manchester, the undisputed capital of cotton manufacturing, although there was still no direct route to Macclesfield. Civil engineer William Baker estimated the construction cost at just £21,900, with £3,100 for land purchase.[35] About twenty-five years later the railway was built to a different plan, with Bollington as an intermediate station between Macclesfield and Marple; Bollington viaduct was the largest structure on the line (Figure 10).[36] If the first approved railway alignment had been adopted, the heart of Bollington would be nothing like it is today and the earlier coming of the railway might have seen Bollington develop into an industrial town of much greater significance.

Conclusion

The early industrial town of Bollington first developed on an east to west axis along a steep-sided river valley, later cut across by huge civil engineering structures that bridge the valley in a north to south direction. The steam-powered cotton mills that followed stand on the plateau on either side of the valley and remain today the dominant man-made features in the area. Towering above the present day urban landscape of Bollington, these monuments to nineteenth-century industry mask the evidence of a late eighteenth-century town once dominated by water power. However, landscape study informed by historical research using a range of sources has enabled that mask to be lifted a little. The early industrial landscape of Bollington is not lost and eighteenth century features can still be discerned by those who take the trouble to seek them out.

References

1. P.P. Burdett, *Survey of the County Palatine of Chester* (1777), with an introduction by J.B. Harley and P. Laxton (Hist. Soc. Lancs. Ches., Occasional series, 1, 1974).
2. W. Marriott, *The Antiquities of Lyme and its Vicinity* (Stockport, 1810), 207–8.
3. 'Map of Bollington, Bosley, Gawsworth, Macclesfield & Rainow', nd, 1611: TNA: MR1/354.
4. 'A Plott of the Prince his Highnes Comons in the Mannor and Forrest of Macclesfield … taken by Edward Maunsell Anno Dom 1611 …': TNA: MPEE1/110.

5. Records of a Court of Survey held for the Manor and Forest of Macclesfield from 3 to 27 Sept. 1611: TNA: LR 2/200, record book, 147–363.
6. J. Laughton, *Seventeenth Century Rainow: the Story of a Cheshire Hill Village* (Leek, 1990).
7. CALS: Will of John Brasier, of Bollington, mason, 1683.
8. Agreement re. Stone delph at Red Hardings, Rainow, 1737: CALS: DDS 37/9.
9. Sale advertisement for property owned by Thomas Birtles in Macclesfield, Hurdsfield, Rainow and Bollington, *London Evening Post*, 5 Oct. 1752.
10. W.H. Shercliffe, D.A. Kitching and J.M Ryan, *Poynton, a Coalmining Village*, chap. 4, (originally published by W. H. Shercliffe, 1983, revised by D.A. Kitching, 2003, published on the personal website of David Kitching, <<http://www.brocross.com/poynton/book/poyco1.htm>>, accessed April 2012); Will of William Clayton of Adlington, coal proprietor, 1851: TNA: PROB 11/2127.
11. S. Bagshaw, *History, Gazetteer and Directory of the County Palatine of Chester* (Sheffield, 1850), 200, 211, 214, 215, 252.
12. E. Hull and A.H. Green, 'The geology of the country around Stockport, Macclesfield, Congleton and Leek', *Memoirs of the Geological Survey of Great Britain* (London, 1866), 10.
13. Advertisement for sale by auction at Knutsford on 18 Nov. 1779 of property in Bollington, the estate of Daniel Orme, *Manchester Mercury & Harrop's General Advertiser*, 16 Nov. 1779.
14. R. Bowling, 'Coal and fireclay mining in the Bollington area', in *When Nancy was Young …* (Bollington Festival Committee, Macclesfield, 1974), 41–48.
15. J. Aikin, *A Description of the Country from Thirty to Forty Miles Round Manchester* (London, 1795), 439.

16. J. Wright, *200 years of Bollington Methodism* (Bollington, 2007), 11.
17. Plan of the Waterhouse Estate in Bollington township, property of Messrs. T.W.C. and J.P. Oliver, esq., 1865, CALS: D2817/50.
18. John Oldham. Unsworn draft statement with respect to mills upstream from Adlington corn mill, *c.*1806: Legh Archives, Adlington Hall: DLA 38/29.
19. Anon., untitled news report of a fire at the Bollington cotton mill of Mr P. Lomas, *London Courier and Evening Gazette*, 22 Nov. 1800.
20. Copy of (a presumed circular) letter to owners and occupiers of cotton mills on the waters flowing to Adlington Mill, 4 Sept. 1807: Legh Archives, Adlington Hall: DLA 38/26.
21. William Richardson. Sworn statement with respect to mills upstream from Adlington corn mill, 8 Aug. 1806, Legh Archives, Adlington Hall: DLA 38/28.
22. G. Longden, *The Industrial Revolution in East Cheshire: Six Theme Walks* (Macclesfield and Vale Royal Groundwork Trust, Bollington, 1988): walk 2, Bollington and Rainow, 10–21; G. Longden, *Bollington in Old Picture Postcards* (European Library, The Netherlands, 1995), 7; G. Longden, 'Kerridge Ridge and Ingersley Vale: A Historical Study' (unpubl., Groundwork Macclesfield and Vale Royal, May 2002).
23. Anon., 'Domestic Intelligence', concerning a fatal accident to William Watts, *The European Magazine and London Review*, L (July–Dec. 1806), 412.
24. Bryant, *Map* (1831).
25. Copy of terms proposed to the township of Shrigley relative to the Highroads, *c.*1793–94, together with a draft

contract and specification for repairs dated 1792: CALS: DDS 444.

26. Anon., 'Scheme for an intended canal navigation from Macclesfield to Mottram Andrew and from thence through Stockport to Manchester, and from the same point in Mottram ... to Northwich', Nov. 1765, within a set of bound pamphlets printed by Thomas Lowndes (London, 1766).

27. B. Outram, 'Report on the proposed Macclesfield Canal', 10 March 1795: reproduced in the *Manchester Gazette & Weekly Advertiser*, 16 April 1796.

28. 'Plan of the intended Macclesfield Canal ... surveyed under the direction of T. Brown', 1811: CALS, plan QDP 26, sections QDP 28.

29. Letters from William Crosley and W. Curie to Thomas Telford, 12 Dec. 1829: West Yorkshire Archives, Wakefield: C299/20/5/1/9.

30. A. Calladine and J. Fricker, *East Cheshire Textile Mills* (RCHM: England, 1993).

31. Lowerhouse Mill (Premises of Slater Harrison Ltd in April 2012), Listing Text, English Heritage Building ID 57918, Grade II Listed 9 Dec. 1983.

32. Minutes of the meeting of the management committee of the Macclesfield Canal Co., 4 Nov. 1835: TNA: RAIL 850/2.

33. Anon., 'Opening of the Macclesfield Branch of the Manchester and Birmingham Railway', *The Manchester Guardian*, 26 Nov. 1845, 6.

34. W. Baker, 'Plan and section of an intended branch railway from the Macclesfield branch railway at or near the Adlington Station to Bollington', Manchester and Birmingham Railway, 1845: CALS: QDP 227.

35. W. Baker, 'Evidence to House of Commons Select Committee on Railway Bills, 15 May 1846', LXVI, 9:

Parliamentary Archives, Westminster: HC/CL/PB/ 2/12/76.
36. B. Jeuda, *The Macclesfield, Bollington and Marple Railway* (Chester, 1983).

9

IN BRIEF

Editors' Introduction

These four short contributions from Society members arise out of poster presentations at the 25th Anniversary Conference. They reflect the wide-ranging interests in, and approaches to, the study of landscape history which the Society seeks to embrace.

The first of these papers is a report on the early stages of a group research project upon which the Society is engaged; a much fuller report will be published in due course. The next two are based on personal research and enquiry into places of interest to individuals. The fourth covers an initiative designed to promote the study of landscape history more widely.

These papers are written in different styles and will provoke different responses. All are testimony to their authors' zeal for the subject and their commitment to sharing it with others.

Selected Field-Names of Cheshire and its Borders
CSLH Field-Names Research Group

Yolk of Egg, Silly Bub Crofts, Little Meadow, Kiln Croft – at first sight field-names may seem quirky or prosaic, fanciful or factual, impossibly obscure or downright dull. But there is always a reason why a patch of land acquires a particular name. It could be the size of the field, the quality of the soil, or the presence of buildings or rural industry. Perhaps it is a feature in the landscape, local fashion or half-forgotten mythology. Alternatively, ownership, tenantry or the whim of a long-dead proprietor may play a part. Some names survive for centuries, others barely a single generation.

Evidence from a wide variety of sources – including local maps, tithe apportionments, diaries, photographs, oral history and land deeds – indicates that Cheshire's field-names exhibit the same diversity of nomenclature found elsewhere in England.

Many medieval field-names survive to this day. In the Victorian tithe apportionments, there are over 150 examples of Cheshire fields named after the number of days' math, or mowing, needed. Across the county a similar number of large medieval fields were divided into quillets (strips). Localised Scandinavian influence can meanwhile be seen in Wirral in names such as Mutler and Mutlowe Field close to the ancient *gemot hlaw* – moot hill, or meeting place – between Brimstage and Thornton Hough.

Documentation from 1767 relating to the land farmed by Robert Pott at Ingersley in Rainow (1767) reveals a preference for names which described the location and character of the land: Higher Meadow, Stoney Flatt, Higher West Clough. The presence of Flatt, incidentally, offers linguistic evidence that east Cheshire was infiltrated by Scandinavian settlers from the Danelaw area of the east midlands.

At Thelwall Eye the former importance of salmon fisheries lingers in names containing the word Laskey (from Old English *leax*, meaning 'salmon', and *eg*, meaning 'island'). Documentary references to Laskey Meadow, House and Lane date back to 1644, though the name was probably in oral use much earlier. The nineteenth-century tithe map shows the larger fields subdivided, but all now lies beneath ship canal dredgings.

Other names are slightly more ambiguous. It is not clear whether Handkerchief Field (1803), situated next to a cotton factory in Bollington, reflects the plot's shape, size, or use as a bleaching field. There are half a dozen examples in Cheshire, not all of which are located near industrial activity.

The chequered progress of some names owes much to local pronunciation. On the Erddig estate Engine Pool – possibly associated with a steam engine – was logged as Indian Pool in early eighteenth-century records. However, when the tithe apportionment was compiled in 1843, there were signs of regression, with Engin Meadow replacing the subcontinental anomaly.

And what of the names mentioned in the first paragraph? Little Meadow and Kiln Croft are straightforward enough. The more imaginative Yolk of Egg signifies a choice piece of land. The name is apparently peculiar to Cheshire, and there are a dozen examples across the county. In Tranmere it may be derived from the yellow local sandstone. Silly Bub Crofts, found in Great Saughall in the parish of Shotwick, is believed to have been derived from sillabub (nowadays usually spelt syllabub) in tribute to lush pasturage with superlative milk yield. If land was fertile, it was clearly considered worth celebrating.

For further information, contact:
fieldnames@cheshirelandscapehistory.org.uk

The Rise and Fall of Llanbedr Hall, near Ruthin (Denbighshire)
Rod Cox

Heraclitus (*c.*535–475 BC) said: 'No man ever steps in the same river twice, for it is not the same river and he is not the same man'. Yet there is continuity: the river itself.

Sixteen 'postcards' were used at the conference to illustrate continuity and change in the landscape surrounding Llanbedr Hall from maps, archaeology, history and legend. Two figures from them are reproduced here.

In the context of Llanbedr Hall (SJ146598) continuity is shown by individual farmsteads along the same contour line, halfway between hilltop and valley floor – the most economic location for livestock farming. Llanbedr's location, on this farm line, suggests ancient roots, but the name originates with the church which was built in a prominent position close to the Roman road. Architecturally the church dates to the thirteenth century yet its name seems older. By the eighteenth century, 70% of the pews were owned by the landowner of Llanbedr reflecting his power in the landscape, for the permanently small congregation suggests a primarily symbolic purpose. The church was closed in 1864 – being rebuilt in a less prominent site – and reduced to a formal ruin in 1896, by which time it had become a folly in the Hall grounds.

Although a hall building is shown on an estate map of 1744, this was replaced by a country house built by Joseph Ablett, cotton magnate, *c.*1770. The parklands were then expanded *c.*1830 when the turnpike closed the Roman road. This huge mansion dominated the vale and continued to do so, even when shoddily re-built in 1866 after a fire: a critically derided 'Seaside Architecture' monument to individual

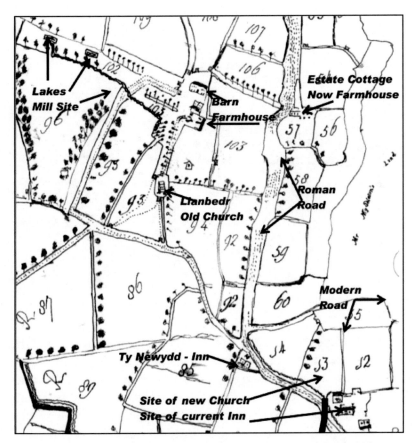

Figure 1. Llanbedr Hall, 1744, a small gentry farm of about 100 acres (original map annotated to show features in the landscape today).

wealth. The 1860s Hall, which survives to this day, contains beams from unknown sixteenth-century buildings, yet it was financed by profits from the Industrial Revolution. It declined after a spendthrift owner died, and was sold with its estate in 1919, like many similar places. The parkland was bought for pasture, a new farm growing from an ex-estate cottage on the 'correct' contour. The bereft Hall was a hospital by 1900, then

255

Figure 2. Llanbedr Hall, *c.*1930, as a TB hospital.

successively became a hotel, nightclub, restaurant and flats. Now, too large for modern commuters, incongruous amongst its neighbours, like an early computer amongst fifty laptops, incapable of modernisation, it is unlisted, ugly. It awaits a planning decision before demolition.

From the Bronze Age, the developing farmed landscape has been the platform on which new economies have placed their Roman forts, Dark Age churches, medieval towns and industries. These economies exploited those local agricultural resources, but Llanbedr Hall depended on remote city industry. Today rural economies depend greatly on money from commuters who buy country houses to escape the cities where they earn it; their houses and gardens are for comfort, not production. One could argue that each of them is Llanbedr Hall written small.

Dawpool Hall Estate, Thurstaston, Wirral: the home of Sir Thomas Henry Ismay, Shipping Magnate

John Lowe

During the latter half of the nineteenth century Liverpool's townscape was expanding on an unprecedented scale, swallowing up the rural landscape and all the villages of the old townships. At the same time the large estates and mansions of the wealthy merchants and ship owners were now engulfed by Victorian urbanisation.[1]

By 1840 the steam ferries were well established and the underground railway was opened in 1886.[2] The more affluent entrepreneurs saw the Wirral Peninsula as an ideal site for their large palatial estates and residences and as a retreat to separate their families from the masses. These super-rich merchant princes and shipping magnates established themselves in grand elegant mansions, landscaped grounds within ringed boundary walls protected by dense woodland and completed with gate lodges. One of the new landowners was the prominent shipping magnate, Thomas Henry Ismay, who moved from Liverpool to Dawpool Hall, Thurstaston.

Dawpool Hall

Ismay's first home, from 1859 to 1865, was 'Enfield House' in Great Crosby, and then he and his family lived at 'Beech Lawn' Waterloo, until in 1884 they moved into the imposing mansion at Dawpool. Thomas Henry Ismay purchased a 390 acre (157.8 hectare) estate in 1877 from the family of the late Joseph Hegan Esq. He demolished the existing house (only built in 1865) and brought in one of the leading architects of the day, Richard Norman Shaw, to create a large mansion at Thurstaston on the Dee shore of Wirral as a replacement. By

Figure 1. An early photograph of Dawpool Hall.

the time the Ismay family moved to Dawpool, Thomas had reached the pinnacle of his professional and public life as one of the most successful ship owners in the world: his White Star Line had a strong and successful Atlantic and Pacific fleet.

The foundation stone of Dawpool was laid in 1882 and the house took over two years to build. All materials used in its construction were of the highest quality, including the finest of the local red sandstone from Heswall Hill. The house was based on an Elizabethan manor house, with sixty rooms and a staff of thirty-two indoor servants. The south front overlooking the Dee was over 250 feet long. The house was completed at a cost of over £53,000.[3]

Ismay's Impact on the Surrounding Landscape
Following completion of the new mansion Thomas Henry Ismay made sure that his new home was not disturbed by the main Heswall and West Kirby road and the railway. He paid out of his own money for a new bypass known as 'Ismay's Cutting'[4] to be constructed. He used his power as a director of the new railway company to move the proposed railway line from his estate to a mile away on the edge of the Dee shore. To

this present day the disused railway track is now the popular Wirral Way: if Ismay had not got his way there would be no walk way and bike ride today.

References
1. A. Lees, *The Hurricane Port: A Social History of Liverpool* (Edinburgh, 2011); Q. Hughes, *Liverpool: City of Architecture* (Liverpool, 1999); K. Parrott, *Village Liverpool* (Liverpool, 2009); English Heritage, *Ordinary Landscapes, Special Places – Anfield, Breckfield and the Growth of Liverpool's Suburbs* (Swindon, 2008).
2. W.R.S. McIntyre, *Birkenhead – Yesterday and Today* (Liverpool, 1948), 19–24.
3. I. and M. Boumphrey, *Yesterday's Wirral No.6* (Prenton, 1991), 44–45; G. Dawson, *Wirral Bits and Bobs* (Irby, 2005), 18–25.
4. G. Dawson, 'Dawpool Hall and Estate: where men moved road and rail', *Wirral Journal*, XV:3 (Autumn 2010), 3–7.

Lifelong Learning
Julie E. Smalley
CSLH Lifelong Learning Co-ordinator

'Lifelong Learning' is the newest activity added to the Society's range of lectures, field trips, newsletter and publications. Most similar groups now have Education as a component of their activity. Expertise already exists amongst CSLH members, at a sizeable yet largely unknown quantity. With this in mind, it made sense to have a vehicle for spreading around the know-how. This could most usefully be exploited through fieldwork recognition and skills development aspects of landscape history.

The 25th Anniversary Conference therefore displayed a Lifelong Learning Poster headed 'Historic Environment – Landscape, Society and Heritage'. By announcing aims of 'promoting interest, pooling expertise, running events and moving forward' the idea was to boost the role of continuing education within our specific context. Under this banner, attendees were invited to consider the potential these themes had to exercise the mind. In other words, Lifelong Learning can be so good for you!

For CSLH members the first Lifelong Learning event was an innovative 'Discovery Day' held in July 2011 in the central Cheshire town of Middlewich, a brief review forming the second part of the Poster. The Saturday workshop was devised to help sharpen observation and interpretation skills. Intended outcome was to learn how to 'read' local landscapes or – for the many 'improvers' amongst the group – learn how to read local landscapes even *better*.

From a convenient base indoors members freely explored the physical townscape, following all or any of three custom-made, self-guided trails with maps. Observed features and any anomalies were to be considered and explained. A plenary session allowed for joint reporting and discussing findings. Those taking part could thus do real landscape history for themselves. An additional tabletop display at the Conference recreated documentary sources made available to view at Discovery Day.

'2012 – and BEYOND' was the third section, indicating more opportunities to enhance field skills for members and possibly the wider community too. Further Discovery Days in differing locations were anticipated. Finally, a request was made to send in comments, responses or suggestions to the Lifelong Learning Co-ordinator, care of the Society. Judging by remarks made on the day, the thirst for more and more usable knowledge on landscape history is nowhere near quenched.

Further information can be found by contacting:
lifelonglearning@cheshirelandscapehistory.org.uk

INDEX OF PLACES

Claverton (Ches.) 112
Clotton (Ches.) 113–14, 125–26, 161
Cockfield (co. Durh.) 66–67
Combermere Abbey (Ches.) 19
Cotton Edmunds (Ches.) 119

Dawpool Hall (Ches.) 5, 257–59
Dean, River 228, 234–36, 241, 242
Dee, River 113, 137, 220, 257–58
Delamere Forest 124–25
Duddon (Ches.) 113, 125, 126, 140, 217
Dudley (Worcs.) 181

Edge (Ches.) 117
Ellesmere (Shrops.) 182
Erddig, Wrexham (Denb.) 252

Farndon (Ches.) 113, 222
Fenemere (Shrops.) 171, 174, 180, 183
Foulk Stapleford (Ches.) 5, 139–42, 144–45, 146, 148, 149, 150, 162
Frodsham (Ches.) 73, 118, 127, 215

Gowy, River 5, 16, 23, 24, 135–37, 139, 140, 145, 147–49, 162

Hadlow (Ches.) 59, 61–64, 72–75, 158
Handbridge (Ches.) 112
Heswall (Ches.) 117, 127, 258
Hockenhull (Ches.) 140, 192
Horton (Ches.) 112, 117, 127
Hurdsfield (Ches.) 232, 233
Huxley (Ches.) 111, 137–38

INDEX OF SUBJECTS